CONFLICT
OF
INTEREST

CONFLICT

OF

INTEREST

A Theory of Divergent Goals with Applications to Politics

ROBERT AXELROD
University of California, Berkeley

Markham Publishing Company/Chicago

MARKHAM POLITICAL SCIENCE SERIES
AARON WILDAVSKY, EDITOR

AXELROD, *Conflict of Interest: A Theory of Divergent Goals with Applications to Politics*

BARBER, *Citizen Politics: An Introduction to Political Behavior*

BARBER, ed., *Readings in Citizen Politics: Studies of Political Behavior*

CNUDDE and NEUBAUER, eds., *Empirical Democratic Theory*

COPLIN, ed., *Simulation in the Study of Politics*

GREENSTEIN, *Personality and Politics: Problems of Evidence, Inference and Conceptualization*

LANE, *Political Thinking and Consciousness: The Private Life of the Political Mind*

LYDEN and MILLER, eds., *Planning-Programming-Budgeting: A Systems Approach to Management*

RANNEY, ed., *Political Science and Public Policy*

RUSSETT, ed., *Economic Theories of International Politics*

SHARKANSKY, *Public Administration: Policy-making in Government Agencies*

SHARKANSKY, ed., *Policy Analysis in Political Science*

STRICKLAND, WADE, and JOHNSTON, *A Primer of Political Analysis*

© MARKHAM PUBLISHING COMPANY 1970
PRINTED IN U.S.A.
LIBRARY OF CONGRESS CATALOG CARD NUMBER: 77-85974
STANDARD BOOK NUMBER: 8410-3020-0

To My Parents

Preface

This study employs mathematical reasoning at a number of points. But fear not. All that is expected of the reader is a vague recollection of high school algebra and geometry. For example, the area of a triangle is one half its base times its height. The occasional uses of mathematics of a more advanced nature are banished to the footnotes, and are not needed for an understanding of the argument.

In the first three chapters, I have borrowed from my earlier article "Conflict of Interest: An Axiomatic Approach," published in *The Journal of Conflict Resolution,* Vol. 11, No. 1, March, 1967, pages 87–99. A comparison will show that a new form of the additivity property has been used and several numerical errors have been corrected. The ideas for the chapter on bureaucracy (Chapter 6) were developed after working summers in the Office of the Secretary of Defense, the Bureau of the Budget, and The RAND Corporation (the last on a project dealing with decisionmaking in bureaucracies). Of course, none of these organizations bears any responsibility for the ideas presented in this study.

This study was submitted to the Department of Political Science of Yale University as my doctoral dissertation, and the work was completed at the University of California at Berkeley.

I owe a debt of thanks to literally dozens of professors and graduate students who have criticized earlier versions of these chapters. Although they cannot all be listed here I would be remiss if I did not acknowledge the sustained help from Professor Hayward Alker, my dissertation advisor at Yale, Professor Martin Shubik of Yale, and Nicholas Miller, my research assistant at Berkeley. While the credit may be shared, the blame is deservedly all mine.

R.A.

June, 1969
Berkeley, California

Contents

Part I

THEORY

1

Conflict of Interest
as a Political Problem

A. Meaning and Utility of the Concept

MEANING OF CONFLICT OF INTEREST

One Saturday morning, with all the summer world bright and fresh, Tom Sawyer was charged by Aunt Polly with the task of whitewashing the fence.

> He began to think of the fun he had planned for this day, and his sorrows multiplied. . . . At this dark and hopeless moment an inspiration burst upon him! . . .
>
> He took up his brush and went tranquilly to work. Ben Rogers hove in sight presently—the very boy, of all boys, whose ridicule he had been dreading. Ben's gait was the hop-skip-and-jump—proof enough that his heart was light and his anticipations high. He was eating an apple, and giving a long melodious whoop, at intervals, followed by a deep-toned ding-dong-dong, ding-dong-dong, for he was personating a steamboat. . . .

Tom went on whitewashing—paid no attention to the steamboat. . . .

Tom's mouth watered for the apple, but he stuck to his work. Ben said:

"Hello, old chap, you got work, hey?"

Tom wheeled suddenly and said:

"Why it's you, Ben! I warn't noticing."

"Say—*I'm* going in a-swimming, *I* am. Don't you wish you could? But of course you'd druther *work*—wouldn't you? Course you would!"

Tom contemplated the boy a bit, and said:

"What do you call work?"

"Why ain't *that* work?"

Tom resumed his whitewashing, and answered carelessly:

"Well, maybe it is, and maybe it ain't. All I know, is, it suits Tom Sawyer."

"Oh, come, now, you don't mean to let on that you *like* it?"

The brush continued to move.

"Like it? Well, I don't see why I oughtn't to like it. Does a boy get a chance to whitewash a fence every day?"

That put the thing in a new light. . . .

"Say, Tom, let *me* whitewash a little."

Tom considered, was about to consent; but he altered his mind:

"No—no—I reckon it wouldn't hardly do, Ben. You see, Aunt Polly's awful particular about this fence—right here on the street, you know—but if it was the back fence I wouldn't mind and *she* wouldn't. . . ."

"Oh, shucks, I'll be just as careful. Now lemme try. Say—I'll give you the core of my apple."

"Well, here—No, Ben, now don't. I'm afeared—"

"I'll give you *all* of it!"

Tom gave up the brush with reluctance in his face, but alacrity in his heart.   (Twain, 1876, Chapter 2)[1]

Tom's success was due to his ability to change Ben's preferences and thereby lower the level of conflict of interest in the situation. Before Tom's inspiration, both boys would have greatly preferred the apple to the whitewashing of the fence. Their goals were incompatible since each wanted the apple, and each would have preferred the other to paint the fence. But Tom was able to change Ben's preferences

---

[1] Full citations are given in the Bibliography. The parenthetical statements within the text refer to the year of publication of the references. Where the material was excerpted from specific pages, those page numbers will also be given. If two works by one author were published in the same year, they will be differentiated in this way: 1967a, 1967b.

so their goals were no longer completely incompatible. Once Ben came to value the whitewashing over the apple, they were able to bargain and arrive at the mutually advantageous trade of Ben's apple for Tom's control over the paintbrush. The trade was an easy one to arrange because the situation had relatively little conflict of interest left in it.

In thinking about conflict of interest, two extreme situations can be visualized: the first has total conflict of interest and the second has no conflict of interest. The kind of situation that has total conflict of interest is an interaction in which whatever one participant wins the other must lose. Interactions of this type are called two-person zero-sum games. They have no room for cooperation and have complete conflict of interest. In the opposite kind of situation, which can be called a partnership game, both participants can attain their most preferred outcome at the same time. Partnership games have no conflict of interest because there is no reason for the participants not to cooperate fully with each other.

If a situation were practically a zero-sum game, one would expect the actors to behave in different ways than if the situation were almost a partnership game. In other words, *the amount of conflict of interest in a situation of strategic interaction can be used to predict certain aspects of the behavior of the actors in that situation.* This study will be a formalization of and elaboration on this basic theme.

Before discussing how this theme will be dealt with, a closer look at the meaning of conflict of interest is in order. An informal definition of conflict of interest which will serve as a point of departure is *the state of incompatibility of the goals of two or more actors.* As such, conflict of interest is a property of the preferences of the participants and the structure of the situation in which they find themselves. It does not refer to their behavior or to the actual outcome of the interaction. The basic theme is that the amount of conflict of interest in a situation affects the behavior of the actors and thus the outcome. It can be regarded as a working hypothesis, a suggestion about how the investigation should proceed. From this theme specific hypotheses will be developed and, where appropriate data are available, the specific hypotheses will be tested by empirical results. Strictly speaking, however, what is tested is not a formal measure of conflict of interest (since such a measure is just a stipulative definition) but rather the theory that people's behavior changes in situations with varying amounts of conflict of interest. Whatever validity such a measure itself has rests upon the extent to which it coincides with what is normally meant by the term "conflict of interest," or "the amount of incompatibility of the players' preferences in a given situation of strategic interaction."

The term "conflict of interest" has been chosen to signify the incompatibility of the goals of two or more actors because it is the term most widely used to represent this concept (see for example Luce and Raiffa, 1957, 1). Although some people prefer "conflict of interests" because more than one interest is in conflict, the other term seems to be more common and will therefore be used in this study. With either spelling, a sharp distinction should be made between the state of incompatibility of the goals of two or more actors and the other usage of the term "conflict of interest," which is exemplified by a government official who engages in illegal private dealings. It should be clear by now that this study uses the term "conflict of interest" in the former sense only.

PURPOSE OF THIS RESEARCH

The amount of conflict of interest in a given situation is important in two respects: as a key explanatory variable, and as a dependent variable of significance in its own right. Using conflict of interest to predict behavior in a wide variety of political arenas will help demonstrate that the concept may be useful as part of a general theory of politics.

The analysis of a specific political activity in terms of conflict of interest serves four functions. First, a formal analysis in terms of conflict of interest provides a new way of looking at a political arena such as the Congressional conference committee. This is useful because it poses old questions in new ways, it raises new questions, and it suggests what new measurements are needed to answer these questions. Second, an analysis in terms of conflict of interest helps answer some old theoretical questions, such as why societies with cross-cutting cleavages are expected to be more stable than societies with overlapping cleavages. Third, such analysis leads to the formulation and testing of new hypotheses. Finally, the analysis of a political activity of one arena in terms of conflict of interest suggests new ways of comparing that activity to the activity of other arenas.

At work here is the law of the instrument: give a small boy (or a researcher) a hammer and he will find things that need hammering. As Kaplan (1964, 29) points out, often the problem is not that some techniques are pushed to the utmost, but that others may, in consequence, be ignored.

SCOPE OF THE PROJECT

The limitations of the investigation should be clearly understood from the outset. The preferences of the players (i.e., their utility schedules) are used to define conflict of interest in a situation with a given strategic structure, and the conflict of interest is used in turn to predict the conflictful behavior of the players. This focus does not include a theory of how utilities are determined in the first place, and does not even consider whether they may in fact be influenced by the players' previous behavior. The utilities are simply taken as given, and the players are assumed to know each other's utilities. Behavior is predicted from conflict of interest, but there is no claim that conflict of interest is the only cause of conflictful behavior. Examples of other causes of conflictful behavior include misperceptions of the situation due to uncertainty (Rappoport, 1965); verbal misunderstandings which form the semanticist conception of conflict (Bernard, 1957, 40f.); aggressive impulses which seek expression no matter what the object (Coser, 1956, 49ff); method of recruitment of experimental subjects (Oskamp and Perlman, 1965); age, sex, class, and race differences (Sampson and Kardush, 1965); and personality factors (Lutzker, 1960). Thus, when behavior is predicted from conflict of interest alone there is an implicit *ceteris paribus* assumption, which means that other things are held equal as conflict of interest is varied.

There are three other aspects of any strategic interaction which are likely to affect the results and which are not directly taken into account by conflict of interest:

1. Possibility of communication. This refers to whether or not the players are free to communicate with each other. It also refers to whether the players can make binding commitments to each other, or whether their pledges can be broken with little or no cost.

2. Complexity of the situation. Two players may have little conflict of interest but still have difficulty cooperating if the situation contains so many details that an agreement is difficult to arrange. However, two factors that reduce the negative effects of complexity are the simplifying assumptions that decisionmakers use in analyzing their task (March and Simon, 1958, and Cyert and March, 1963) and the existence of salient options which help the players achieve tacit coordination (Schelling, 1960).

3. Relevance of the interaction. Not all strategic interactions in which a player takes part are important to him. As Karl Deutsch (1966, 303) points out, the relations between Thailand and Bolivia are not likely to be crucial to either one of them because they are so remote from one another.

Conflict of interest can also be regarded as a contextual variable suitable for incorporation into other theories of interpersonal behavior.

For example, the effects of personality and conflict of interest might be additive. In other words, some people are less predisposed to co-operation than others, and some situations are less conducive to co-operation than others. So an uncooperative person in a high conflict of interest situation is very likely to display conflictful behavior. Ideally the various explanations of behavior could be integrated so that the *ceteris paribus* assumption of each separate theory could be eliminated.

OUTLINE OF THE STUDY

The rest of this chapter consists of a review of the literature rele-vant to conflict of interest, and an examination of the contribution of game theory to the study of strategic interaction. The next chapter is written as a conversation between an *Empiricist,* a *Theoretician* and a *Practical Man* in order to develop the meaning and significance of conflict of interest in the context of bargaining. The third chapter extends the analysis to the dilemma of collective action and uses labora-tory data to test a number of specific hypotheses about the effects of conflict of interest on behavior.   The final chapter of Part I discusses how the concept can be applied to the study of actual political arenas.

Part II applies the theory of conflict of interest to a number of political processes. The first application, given in Chapter 5, is to the bargaining process in the Congressional conference committee. The sixth chapter examines the multilevel decision process characteristic of bureaucracies. Spatial models of society are used in the seventh chapter to treat the subject of conflict and consensus. The eighth chapter explores the process of coalition formation and maintenance.

The concluding section reviews the progress made in the use of the concept of conflict of interest, and describes those research problems relating to conflict of interest which remain unsolved.

B. Review of the Literature

CONFLICT OF INTEREST IN THE SOCIAL SCIENCES

The concept of conflict of interest is found almost everywhere and practically nowhere. Almost everywhere in the sense that "In all of man's written record there has been a preoccupation with conflict of interest; possibly only the topics of God, love, and inner struggle have received comparable attention" (Luce and Raiffa, 1957, 1). Practically nowhere in the sense that few people have attempted to formalize the notion of incompatible goals or apply it in a systematic way to empirical data.

Conflict of interest is close to the heart of political science. Aristotle, Rousseau, and Madison are just a few of those who were deeply concerned with this concept, and several of their contributions are discussed as political applications in Part II. However, a comprehensive treatment of their thinking is beyond the scope of the present study. Modern political scientists also regard conflict of interest as near the heart of politics. As Dahl (1963, 72) put it: "Let one person frustrate another in the pursuit of his goals, and you already have the germ of a political system." Easton (1965, 48) is equally emphatic: "Conflicts over demands constitute the flesh and blood of all political systems, from the smallest to the largest and from the simplest to the most complex." The very existence of power requires conflict of interest between the participants (Bachrach and Baratz, 1963). As a final statement on the centrality of conflict of interest for political science, consider Mayo's formulation:

> Robinson Crusoe is much beloved of economic theory, but he is no use at all to political theory until Friday comes on the scene. Political relations arise when men agree on some things and disagree on others, when there is some compatibility and some conflict, both common and conflicting interests, both partnership and competition, out of which a binding policy is to be shaped. (1960, 6)

Several other disciplines are almost as assertive about their relationship to the problems of conflict of interest. Boulding makes the claim for economics:

> The fundamental characteristic of an issue conflict is that there should be scarcity of some desired resource or good, in the sense that I have sometimes facetiously called the *Duchess's Law*—after its classical statement in Alice in Wonderland, "the more there is of yours, the less there is of mine"—dominates the situation. Scarcity, however, is the peculiar province of the economist and hence we would not be surprised to find concepts of conflict at the very center of economics. (1965, 172)

Bernard speaks for sociologists when she says (1957, 38), "Implicit in the sociological conceptualization of conflict is some theory of cost. Conflict arises when there are incompatible or mutually exclusive goals or aims or values espoused by human beings."

DEFINITION

Everyone talks about conflict of interest, but few people do much about it.   The first problem, of course, is to devise a working definition.   The most common definition is the informal one adopted here: the state of incompatibility of the goals of two or more actors.   Among those who use this or similar formulations are Morton Deutsch (1949, 132), Bernard (1957, 38), Aubert (1963, 27), Berelson and Steiner (1964, 588), and Porsholt (1966, 179). Karl Deutsch adds to incompatibility of goals the cost of avoiding collision (1963, 112). But few researchers are any more explicit than this about how conflict of interest can be formalized.   Many do not even clearly distinguish between the sources of conflictful behavior, such as conflict of interest, and the behavior itself.   A striking example of this is Georg Simmel's famous work *Conflict,* which is   sympathetically and fully treated by Coser (1956).

Several investigators have attempted to specify the amount of conflict of interest in a situation of strategic interaction, but have treated only limited aspects of the problem.   The one approach which deals with the problem in its entirety is that of Rapoport and his colleagues (1960), (1962), (1965), (1967a).   Since their work refers to only one type of strategic interaction (the Prisoner's Dilemma), an examination of their work is best postponed until the third chapter where this type of interaction is treated.   Three other approaches will now be considered.

The first approach deals with a single move.   Boulding (1965, 190) defines the *coefficient of conflict* of a move as the loss to one party per unit gain of the other.   For example, if player A gives up two units of his welfare so that player B can gain six units the coefficient of conflict for that move is one-third.   The less A sacrifices to help B by a given amount, the lower is the coefficient of conflict for that move.   A closely related idea is the *ease of being generous.*   Pruit (1965) defines this as the inverse ratio, i.e., the gain to one party per unit cost to the other.   So if B gains six units due to A's sacrifice of two units, the ease of A's being generous to B is 3.   If some moves have a higher coefficient of conflict (and a lower ease of being generous) than others, no single number can be assigned to the situation before the players decide what move to make.   And what if the result of a decision by A depends on the simultaneous strategy choice made by B?   In that case, A's ease of generosity to B cannot be determined from A's choice alone.   Thus these two concepts are insufficient to measure conflict of interest because they refer to a given move by a single player rather than to the whole range of strategy choices open to both players simultaneously. They are useful ways to think about one aspect of the problem, however, and in general one might conjecture that in some sense the easier it is for one player to be generous to another, the less conflict of interest there is. This conjecture will be considered again later.

The second approach uses expected gain. Churchman (1961, 309f.) says the *degree to which A conflicts with B* is the expected gain to B of A's not achieving his goal.[2] Ackoff (1965) calls the *conflict seen by a decisionmaker* the expected gain to the decisionmaker which would result from the other participants also attempting to control the environment.[3] (If the entry of others hinders the first decisionmaker, the conflict he sees has a negative value.) To use either of these concepts one must know the probability of each player selecting each choice in a given situation of strategic interaction; otherwise the amount of expected gain cannot be determined. But any scheme based on complete knowledge of everyone's behavior in the interaction itself cannot be used to predict that same behavior. Therefore this approach is not useful for a test of the basic theme that predicts that the more conflict of interest there is in a situation the more likely it is that conflictful behavior will result. What is needed is a measure of conflict of interest based solely on the utilities of the players and the structure of the situation.

---

[2] Here are the details. The degree to which A conflicts with B is defined as

$$V_B \cdot [P(O_B/ - O_A,N) - P(O_B/O_A,N)]$$

where V_B is the value (utility) of B's goal O_B for B, $P(O_B/ - O_A,N)$ is the probability that O_B will occur given that O_A does not occur in the environment (N), and $P(O_B/O_A,N)$ is the same probability given that O_A does occur.

The expected value of an event is just its value times the probability that it will occur. The degree to which A conflicts with B is the expected value to B if A does not attain his goal minus the expected value to B if A does. Therefore the degree to which A conflicts with B is the gain in the expected value to B of A's not getting his goal.

[3] The conflict seen by a decisionmaker is defined as

$$DC_r = \Sigma_i \Sigma_j P_i E_{ij} U_j - \Sigma_i \Sigma_j P_i \bar{E}_{ij} U_j$$

where P_i is the probability r will choose i, E_{ij} is the probability j will result if i is chosen, with the other decisionmakers attempting to control the environment, $\bar{E}_{ij}$ is the same probability in the absence of the other decisionmakers, and U_j is the value of j to r.

Note that the expected value to r of a choice i is just $\Sigma_j P_i E_{ij} U_j$ or $\Sigma_j P_i \bar{E}_{ij} U_j$ depending on the presence or absence of other decisionmakers. Therefore DC_r is the expected gain to the decisionmaker which would result from the other participants also attempting to control the environment.

The third approach is based solely on the utilities of the players, but without regard to the structure of the situation. The most specific formulation is by Reich (1968), although the basic idea is contained in Karl Deutsch's term "covariance of rewards or interests" (1966, 302). The problem with this approach is that it regards all outcomes as strategically equivalent and does not take into account the relationships between the strategy choices of the players and the various outcomes.

An example will illustrate how the covariance approach can fail to provide a good indication of the amount of conflict of interest in a situation. Suppose that in a strategic interaction there are a large number of possible outcomes and the two players rank the outcomes in exactly the opposite order of preference. Such a situation clearly has high conflict of interest. But now suppose that a single new possible outcome is added which both players prefer to all of the old possible outcomes. In the new situation all the conflict of interest has disappeared because the players will have no difficulty in jointly selecting the mutually optimal outcome, now that one exists. However, the covariance of all the possible outcomes will not have changed very much because only one new possible outcome has been added to the many old ones. The concept of covariance treats the new outcome as just one more possible outcome among many and indicates that not much has changed. Yet the interaction has changed completely, from one of high conflict of interest to one of no conflict of interest at all. Thus an adequate measure of conflict of interest must be based not only on the utilities of the players but also on the structure of the situation.

HYPOTHESES

After the problem of defining conflict of interest comes the question of what hypotheses and predictions can be made that use this concept. The main theme of this study is that the greater the conflict of interest the more likely is conflictful behavior. Several other researchers would seem to agree with this broad formulation, provided it is understood that the participants are aware of the conflict of interest between them. For example, Lasswell (1931, 194) says "Social conflict results from the conscious pursuit of exclusive values" and, as already noted, Bernard (1957, 38) says "Conflict arises when there are incompatible goals or aims or values espoused by human beings." Finally, in regard to international negotiations, Sawyer and Guetzkow (1965, 467) caution against the view that "international conflict arises simply from misperception and misunderstanding; on the contrary, conflict appears to result in large part from objective incompatibility of goals among states." Note that like many other authors, the ones quoted here use the term "conflict" to mean conflictful behavior. This is not done in this study in order to keep clear the distinction between conflict of interest and conflictful behavior, a distinction which is often blurred in the literature.

An apparent dissent to the basic theme is advanced by Harsanyi, but as we shall see the difference is not great. Harsanyi's point is worth quoting at length.

> A conflict of interest does not explain an active behavioral conflict, because both sides could benefit by accepting some compromise solution which would enable them to restore full cooperation in matters affecting their common interests, thereby saving the costs of an active conflict. Hence, observed active conflicts between different social classes or other social groups require explanations going beyond the mere existence of a partial conflict of interest. The explanations must include mutual distrust because there is no mechanism for enforcing agreements, unrealistic extreme demands by one or both sides caused by misjudgment of their relative power positions, failure to understand common interests, sheer emotional hostility, enjoyment of a conflict for its own sake, etc. (1966, 14)

To see why the basic theme is consistent with this argument, two points made earlier need to be recalled. First, conflict of interest is not supposed to be the only cause of conflictful behavior, but only one possible cause among many. Thus the explanations offered by Harsanyi are all useful supplements to a discussion of conflictful behavior in terms of conflict of interest. Second, since nearly all social interactions involve some conflict of interest, it is quite accurate to say that "A conflict of interest does not explain an active behavioral conflict. . . ." But if some procedure were available to measure just how much conflict of interest existed, then the amount of conflict of interest might indeed explain (at least in part) the conflictful behavior. Thus, if there are two situations which differ solely in the amount of conflict of interest they contain, and if the one with the greater conflict of interest does in fact also exhibit more conflictful behavior, then there can be no doubt that the relative amount of conflict of interest can be used to explain the difference in conflictful behavior. In other words, Harsanyi's point of view is a useful reminder that the basic theme must be regarded as applying when "other things are equal" and must be interpreted as providing the basis for comparing the amount of conflict of interest in one situation to that in another.

Another useful point is May and Doob's proposition (1937, 23) that "human beings by original nature strive for goals, but striving with others (cooperation) or against others (competition) are learned forms of behavior." An important corollary is that the validity of predictions concerning conflictful behavior are likely to be culturally dependent.

The basic theme is, of course, a highly generalized formulation that must be made much more specific before it can be tested in a particular context. Two studies that provide many propositions more specific than the general theme are by Morton Deutsch (1949) and Lewis Coser (1956). Both of these are primarily concerned with sociological variables, such as group solidarity. There is also a body of political science literature on consensus and cleavage in societies which deals explicitly with the effects of different levels of conflict of interest. This literature of pluralism applies to the societal level and does not (for example) refer to either collegial bodies or international relations. Therefore it is discussed in Chapter 7 where societal conflict of interest is treated.

SUMMARY OF THE ISSUES

This brief review of the social science literature has served to highlight a number of issues relating to the definition and use of the concept of conflict of interest. Although no procedure seems to exist which can measure the amount of conflict of interest in a situation, we have seen that:

1. Conflict of interest refers to the whole range of strategy choices open to all the players, not just to a given choice by one of them.
2. Conflict of interest must be defined independently of the behavior it is used to predict.
3. Conflict of interest is sensitive to the structure of an interaction as well as to the preferences of the players.

With respect to the basic theme that conflict of interest leads to conflictful behavior, we have seen that:

1. This assumes the participants are aware there is conflict of interest between them.
2. The basic theme also contains an implicit *ceteris paribus* assumption.
3. An important corollary of this point is that predictions about conflictful behavior are likely to be culturally dependent.

	B_1	B_2
A_1	1,1	1,10
A_2	10,1	0,0

Game 1
High Conflict
of Interest

	B_1	B_2
A_1	9,9	9,10
A_2	10,9	0,0

Game 2
Low Conflict
of Interest

FIGURE 1-1

4. To be useful as an explanation of conflictful behavior, the amount of conflict of interest must be comparable from one situation to another.

C. The Contribution of Game Theory

STRATEGIC INTERACTION

We have seen that conflict of interest refers to the whole range of choices open to all the players simultaneously. For this reason, the elementary concepts of game theory provide an excellent framework in which to formalize a discussion of conflict of interest.

These concepts are simple enough. In a game, two or more players each have a set of choices called strategies. Simultaneously each player selects one of his strategies, and together these strategy choices determine the outcome. The outcome provides each player with a payoff.

A strategic interaction is reduced to its barest fundamentals by this formulation, and that is the primary contribution of game theory to a study of conflict of interest and conflictful behavior. For example, compare the two games in Figure 1-1. In both games, the two players, A and B, each have two strategies. Player A can select either row A_1 or row A_2 and player B can select either column B_1 or column B_2. The outcome is given by payoffs entered in the appropriate cell of the matrix. By convention, the payoff to the row-chooser is entered first. Thus, in the first game if A chooses the second row and B chooses the first column, A gets 10 units of his utility and B gets one of his.

What is the strategic situation in these two games? In the first game, A can either play it safe by selecting the first row and be sure of getting one unit, or he can hope that B selects the first column and try for 10 units with a chance of getting none. From B's point of view the game is the same: he can be sure of getting one unit by selecting the first column, or he can select the second column which yields 10 points or none depending on whether A selects the first or second row. An interesting feature of many games, including this one, is its revolving logic: what the first player should do depends on what the second player does, but what the second player should do depends on what the first player does. But what the first player should do depends on what the second player does, and so on, forever.

The strategic situation in the second game is exactly the same, except that each player can get nine units for sure (rather than one) by using his first strategy.

What about the incompatibility of the goals of the players in these games? In both games, each player can get 10 units, provided that the other player does not try for 10. In other words, one player's attempt to get 10 units precludes the other from also getting 10. If both try for their maximum, both get nothing. Thus there is some incompatibility in both games. However, the incompatibility of the second game is not as severe because there both players can at the same time get almost their maximum payoffs. There is not nearly as strong an incentive as there is in the first game for either player to try his second strategy and thereby block the possibility of the other player's getting his maximum payoff. Therefore the pressure on both to select their second strategy and thereby block each other's success is less strong in the second game. In brief, the second game has less conflict of interest. This is still a long way from formalizing the notion of conflict of interest, but it does illustrate the important point that the amount of conflict of interest in a situation of strategic interaction depends on the payoff matrix. As we shall see in Chapter 3, conflict of interest also depends on whether the players are allowed to communicate and make binding agreements.

UTILITY THEORY

If numbers are to be put in the payoff matrix, it is necessary to measure each player's utility.[4] The following procedure of determining the utility of an outcome has been provided by Von Neumann and Morgenstern (1947). Suppose a person prefers X to Y and Y

---

[4] For many purposes it is sufficient to know only the ordinal ranking of a player's preferences. See Chapter 4.

to Z, and suppose that the utility of X is arbitrarily set equal to one and the utility of Z arbitrarily set equal to zero. Now, there exists a unique number p between 0 and 1 which represents the point at which a person is indifferent between (a) getting Y for sure, and (b) a lottery with a p chance of getting X and a $1 - p$ chance of getting Z. The number p can then be used to measure the utility of Y relative to X and Z. If Y is almost as valued as X then p will be only slightly less than one, and if Y is not much preferred to Z then p will be almost zero.

Two observations should be made about this way of measuring utility. First, the zero and unit points are arbitrary. The utility scale is an interval scale like the scale on a thermometer. The Centigrade scale, for example, uses the freezing and boiling points of water to anchor its scale, but any two points could have been used. It is meaningless to say that 50°C is twice as warm as 25°C. Likewise if $p_Y = .25$ and $p_W = .50$ one could not meaningfully say that W was twice as valued as Y, but an accurate statement is that W is twice as far along from Z to X as Y is. The second observation is that utility is an index of the preferences of the player himself and in theory at least is measured by observing the choices the player makes when confronted with various lotteries. For example, the player may prefer 50 cents to an even chance of getting a dollar (or nothing). Then the utility to him of 50 cents is greater than the average of the utility of a dollar and nothing.

SUBDISCIPLINES OF GAME THEORY

Most of the work in game theory belongs to one of two relatively distinct subdisciplines: (1) formal analysis of what strategy a player will or should select in a given situation, and (2) empirical studies using laboratory experiments to determine the effects variables such as sex, authoritarianism, and wording of the instructions have on the actual play of the game.

This study of conflict of interest differs from that of most of the formal analyses in three regards. First, most hypotheses predict relative frequencies of alternative choices and do not identify the choice or choices that are in some sense distinguished. Second, some of the strongest assumptions used in formal analysis are not employed because they are unrealistic, and for the present purposes are also unnecessarily restrictive. For example, most of the results of this study apply to the trial and error behavior of ordinary people as well as to the behavior of abstract actors who are assumed to be fully calculating and narrowly rational.   Finally, some of the institutional arrangements of specific political arenas are used to construct more concrete models than the highly abstract models used in most formal analyses.

Unlike most empirical studies, the present study is not confined to laboratory situations for observations, and focuses on the effects of changing the entries in the payoff matrix rather than the personality of the players or the conditions of the play.

Now we are ready to see how the notion of conflict of interest can be made precise and how it can be used.

2

Conflict of Interest and Bargaining

Dramatis Personae
  Empiricist
  Theoretician
  Practical Man

A. The Bargaining Problem

Empiricist: So far we have only an informal definition of conflict of interest: the extent of the incompatibility of goals. But what precisely is meant by the phrase "incompatibility of goals?" How can I measure the amount of conflict of interest in a given situation? How can I determine whether the goals of the participants are more incompatible in one situation than another?

Theoretician: These are difficult questions to answer, especially if you want to be able to compare any two games no matter how dissimilar. So let's begin with a particular kind of strategic interaction and examine what conflict of interest means in games of this one type. The kind I have in mind was invented by Nash in 1950 and is called the bargaining game. It's a good type of game to start with because it is conceptually simple and yet contains some of the most important strategic aspects of bargaining.

Let's look at bargaining games and see if we can specify some properties that should be satisfied by any procedure measuring conflict of interest for these games.   If these properties are not very restrictive there will be many possible ways to measure conflict of interest.   On the other hand, if they are too restrictive there will be no procedure that satisfies all of them at once.   The ideal case is a list of reasonable properties restrictive enough to permit no more than one possible procedure, and not so restrictive as to eliminate all procedures.   With such a list there will be one and only one way to measure conflict of interest in bargaining games.

Empiricist: I'm used to measuring things with the procedures at hand, but how did you get the idea of developing a new procedure from a list of reasonable properties?

Theoretician: Nash himself listed some reasonable properties, but he was interested in using his list to determine what the outcome of the game would be rather than to measure the amount of conflict of interest in it.   Actually it was Shannon's axiomatic development in 1949 of a way to measure the amount of information in a message that gave me the idea that a list of reasonable properties might be used to determine how to measure conflict of interest in bargaining games.

Empiricist: Do you actually have such a list in mind?

Theoretician: Yes.

Empiricist: And do you know what is the unique way to measure conflict of interest in bargaining games?

Theoretician: Yes, but let's proceed step by step.   First we will develop the list, and then we will look at the procedure I claim is the one and only one which satisfies each of these properties.

Empiricist: How will I know your procedure works, and how will I know that someone else couldn't invent another procedure which also satisfies all of the properties.

Theoretician: Why, I'll prove it to you of course.   To begin at the beginning, let me tell you what a bargaining game is.   Two players can talk to each other and make binding agreements.   Some agreements are feasible and some are not.   If two agreements are feasible, we shall also assume that any agreement on a random selection between the two is also feasible.   Furthermore, there is a single predetermined outcome which I'll call the *no agreement point* that occurs if no agreement is reached.   In other words, either player can veto anything other than the no agreement point.   Finally, in order for the situation to be a bargaining game there must be something to bargain about, which means that at least one of the feasible outcomes is preferred by both players to the no agreement point.

As a simple example, suppose Andrew has an apple and Orville has an orange and each prefers the other's fruit to his own. Let's ignore the possibility of dividing up either piece of fruit. There are four elementary feasible agreements since there are four ways of distributing the apple and the orange between Andrew and Orville. Andrew and Orville could also agree to each get a million dollars, but this is hardly a feasible outcome. However they can agree to such outcomes as letting Andrew have the apple and flipping a coin to see who gets the orange.

To make the example more specific, let's suppose that Andrew is indifferent between (a) having the apple, and (b) a lottery in which he has one chance in six of getting both fruits and five chances in six of getting neither. In other words, for Andrew the utility of the apple is $\frac{1}{6}$ of the way from neither to both fruits. Let's also suppose that for Andrew the value of the orange is $\frac{5}{6}$ of the way from neither to both. For Orville, we will take the apple to be $\frac{3}{5}$ of the way and the orange to be $\frac{2}{5}$ of the way from neither to both. There are many ways to represent the utility schedules of the two players, but one way which is as good as any other is shown in the table below. You can see that all the necessary relationships hold. For instance, for Andrew the utility of the apple is 3, which is $\frac{1}{6}$ of the way from the utility of getting neither (2) to the utility of getting both (8).

Once we choose a representation for the utility schedules it is easy to draw a graph representing the game. I have done this in Figure 2-1. We already know that the four outcomes of Table 2-1 are not the only ones possible since randomizations are allowed. The players could therefore agree that one of them should get both pieces of fruit, and that they will flip a coin to determine who it is. This outcome (labeled E in Figure 2-1) has a utility of $\frac{1}{2}$ (2) $+ \frac{1}{2}$ (8) $= 5$ for Andrew, and $\frac{1}{2}$ (1) $+ \frac{1}{2}$ (6) $= 3\frac{1}{2}$ for Orville. This agreement is certainly not an efficient one since both can do better. For instance, outcome C gives Andrew 7 and Orville 4. Another feasible agreement

TABLE 2-1

Outcome	Andrew Gets:	Andrew's Utility Is:	Orville Gets:	Orville's Utility Is:
A	Both	8	Neither	1
B*	Apple	3	Orange	3
C	Orange	7	Apple	4
D	Neither	2	Both	6

* No agreement point

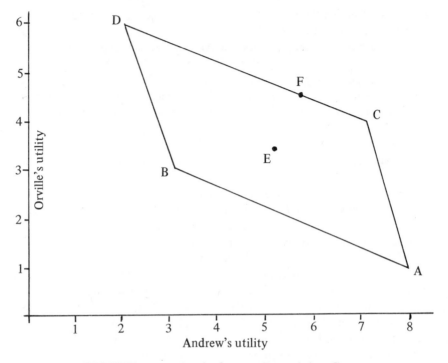

FIGURE 2-1. Apple-Orange Bargaining Game

(F) is a ¾ chance of outcome C and a ¼ chance of outcome D.   To
Andrew the utility of this agreement is ¾ (7) + ¼ (2) = 5¾ and to
Orville it is ¾ (4) + ¼ (6) = 4½.   This too is better for both than
E, but Andrew prefers C to F while Orville prefers F to C.   Outcome
F is efficient (or *Pareto optimal* as it is called) since if one player is
to get more than F gives him, the other player must get less.

     If we plot all the feasible agreements they will fill the region in
Figure 2-1.   An important thing to notice is that the region of feasible
agreements of any bargaining game must be convex since randomizations are allowed.   Also notice that a bargaining game is completely
described by specifying the region of feasible agreements and the no
agreement point.

     Empiricist: Wait a minute.   I am not too clear on what trading
apples and oranges has to do with politics.

     Thoretician: Trading is quite common in politics.   When two
Congressmen logroll they are trading votes, and when two nations compromise on a treaty they may be trading some clauses in one's draft
for some clauses in the other's.   Even when there is no question of

a trade, politics frequently involves trying to improve the status quo by reaching a mutually acceptable agreement.   There is often a common interest in reaching some agreement, but the interests also diverge to some extent over the issue of just which possible outcome will become the actual agreement.   Politics is full of this kind of bargaining.

Even coin-flipping is sometimes used.   When freshmen Senators Edward Brooke and Charles Percy were appointed to the same two committees, *Time* (February 17, 1967) reported that they flipped coins to decide who should have senior ranking.   Brooke won both tosses.

B. Desirable Properties of Conflict of Interest in Bargaining Games

Empiricist: Let's return to my original question: how can I measure conflict of interest?   How much conflict is there, for example, between Andrew and Orville?

Theoretician: I'm ready to begin when you are.

Empiricist: Before you start, let me warn you that any scheme you come up with had better not depend on which player's utility you put on the horizontal axis of the graph, and which on the vertical axis.   If I redraw the game so that Orville's utility is plotted on the horizontal axis and Andrew's on the vertical axis, the amount of conflict of interest should not change.

Theoretician: I promise it.   In fact, let's use this as the first property that should be satisfied by any procedure to measure conflict of interest in bargaining games.   This property of invariance with respect to an interchange of the labels of the players can be called *symmetry*.

Empiricist: There are some other arbitrary choices in the representation of the game, as you yourself pointed out earlier.

Theoretician: Namely?

Empiricist: Namely the particular ways in which the two utility schedules are represented.   Andrew's utility schedule must have the apple $\frac{1}{6}$ of the way from neither to both fruits, and the orange $\frac{5}{6}$ of the way, but there are many ways to do this.   There are also many ways to represent Orville's utility schedule so that the apple is $\frac{3}{5}$ of the way from neither to both and the orange is $\frac{2}{5}$ of the way.   The conflict of interest should be independent of the specific representation which is chosen.

Theoretician: I'll guarantee that too.   Just to have a name for this property, let's call it *independence*.   Now I have promised that my procedure to measure conflict of interest in bargaining games will satisfy symmetry and independence.   What else are you going to make me promise?

Empiricist: I have some notion that if two games are almost the same they ought to have almost the same amount of conflict of interest. For example if Orville regarded the value of the apple to be .61 of the way from neither to both instead of $\frac{3}{5}$ of the way this should not affect the amount of conflict of interest too much.

Theoretician: And if it were .605 it would make even less difference, and .601 would have still less effect on the amount of conflict of interest.

Empiricist: Exactly.

Theoretician: This idea is captured in the concept of equality in the limit. Suppose there is an infinite sequence of games, G_i, each with the same no agreement point as game G. Suppose also that the regions of feasible agreements of these games get to be closer and closer approximations of the region of G so that the limit of the sequence of G_i is exactly the same as G.

Empiricist: Then the conflict of interest of each game in the sequence should be closer and closer to the conflict of interest of the game G, and the limit of the conflicts of interest of G_i must equal the conflict of interest of G.

Theoretician: Fine. Let's call this *continuity*. For a given game, G, and an infinite sequence of games, G_i, with the same no agreement point, if the region of G is the limit of the regions of G_i then the conflict of interest of G is the limit of the conflicts of interest of the games G_i.

Empiricist: That's an elegant way to say what I meant when I wanted similar games to have similar amounts of conflict of interest, so I'm going to ask you to promise that continuity be satisfied too.

Theoretician: It's done. Now I have a small favor to ask of you. Do you mind if I insist that the conflict of interest of every bargaining game be no greater than a given number.

Empiricist: That's fine with me.

Theoretician: It doesn't matter which number I pick since if two procedures differ only in that one gives a value twelve times as large as the other for any game, then these two procedures are for all practical purposes identical, just as inches and feet are equivalent ways to measure length.

Empiricist: How about saying that the game with the most conflict of interest has a conflict of interest of one?

Theoretician: Since it doesn't make any difference which number I select, let me use $\frac{1}{2}$. I have a good reason, but it won't become obvious until later. So the fourth property that must be satisfied by any procedure to measure conflict of interest in bargaining games is *boundedness*. The bargaining game with the most conflict of interest has conflict of interest equal to $\frac{1}{2}$.

TABLE 2-2

Outcome	Doris Gets:	Doris' Utility Is:	Frances Gets:	Frances' Utility Is:
A′	Both	5.5	Neither	2
B′*	Date	3	Fig	3
C′	Fig	5.25	Date	4
D′	Neither	2.5	Both	4.5

* No agreement point

Now we have four properties, and I have just one more in mind. This one will allow us to compare bargaining games that are quite different—provided they bear a certain special relationship to each other. Before discussing this, consider another game in which Doris has a date and Frances has a fig, and once again each prefers the other's fruit to her own. One version of the utility schedules is given in Table 2-2 and the game is plotted in Figure 2-2. The original apple-orange game between Andrew and Orville is repeated in Fig-

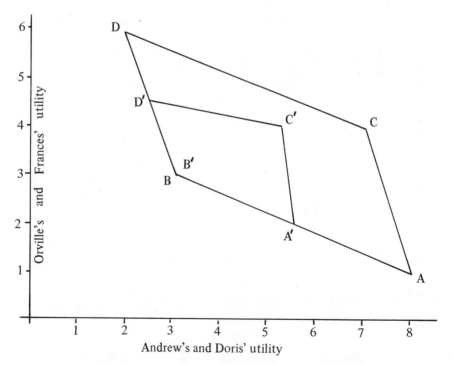

FIGURE 2-2. Apple-Orange and Date-Fig Games

TABLE 2-3

Outcome	Doris Gets:	Doris' Utility Is:	Frances Gets:	Frances' Utility Is:
A′	Both	10.5	Neither	0
B′*	Date	3	Fig	3
C′	Fig	9.75	Date	6
D′	Neither	1.5	Both	7.5

* No agreement point

ure 2-2 for comparison. You can see that the two games have the same no agreement point but that the region of feasible outcomes of the new game is entirely contained in the region of the old game. What would you say about the relative amount of conflict of interest in these two games?

Empiricist: The game with the smaller region appears to have more conflict of interest.

Theoretician: Why?

Empiricist: Because, for any agreement reached in the new game, there would be a feasible outcome in the original game which would be better for both players.

Theoretician: But what if I use a different representation of Doris' and Frances' utility schedules, as in Table 2-3 and Figure 2-3? A minute ago you said that Doris and Frances have more conflict of

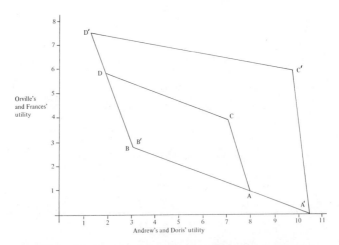

FIGURE 2-3. Apple-Orange Game and Another
Representation of Date-Fig Game

interest than Andrew and Orville because their region is smaller, but now the same reasoning would indicate that Andrew and Orville have more.

Empiricist: I can't have it both ways. Obviously my line of reasoning did not take into account the property of conflict of interest which requires independence with respect to the representation of the utility schedules. Can't we settle on some single representation that would allow a comparison of the games?

Theoretician: That's just what we need. Without it any game could be made to appear to have both more conflict of interest and less conflict of interest than any other game. Now, do you have any suggestion for which representation of the utility schedules to use?

Empiricist: How about setting the zero equal to the worst the player can get, and the unit equal to the best he can get?

Theoretician: That will do nicely. Let's say that a game represented for both players in this form is *normalized*. The worst is obviously the no agreement point since a player can be sure of getting this much by being obstinate. The best a player can hope for is the most desired of those outcomes that the other player is not sure to veto. The other player is sure to veto any proposed agreement that gives him less than what he gets if no agreement is reached. Therefore the best a player can hope for is the most desired of those outcomes that gives the other player at least the same utility as the no agreement point gives him.

For example, let's look at the original game in which Andrew has an apple and Orville has an orange (solid lines in Figure 2-4). The worst Andrew can do is to retain his apple. The best he can hope for is to get Orville to agree to give him a $\frac{1}{3}$ chance of getting both fruits (outcome A) and a $\frac{2}{3}$ chance of getting only the orange (C). This outcome (labeled H in Figure 2-4) is efficient and Andrew cannot hope to get anything more because Orville is already indifferent between this outcome and simply keeping his orange. Likewise Orville's worst is the no agreement point, and his best (outcome I) is a $\frac{4}{5}$ chance of getting both fruits (D) and a $\frac{1}{5}$ chance of getting the orange (C). Therefore the normalized version of the apple-orange game uses the utility schedules shown in graph form in Figure 2-4. The fig–date game is also shown in normalized form in the dotted lines of Figure 2-4.

Empiricist: What about the property that says conflict of interest should be independent of which representation is chosen?

Theoretician: The property of independence guarantees that the conflict of interest of the normalized version of a game is the same

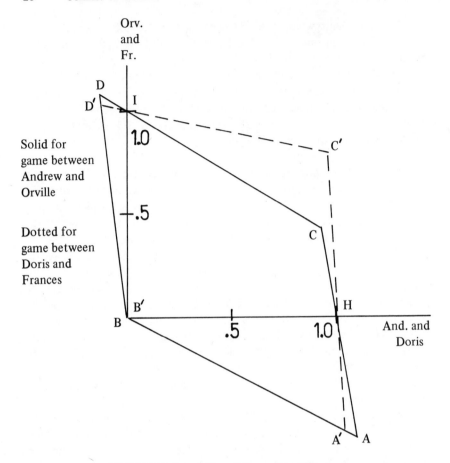

FIGURE 2-4.   Two Normalized Games

as the conflict of interest of any other version of it.   So normalizing a game has no effect on the amount of conflict of interest.   The advantage is that once two games are normalized, they may be easy to compare.

To see how easy the comparison can become, look at Figure 2-4. Only the part of the region of feasible agreements which is above and to the right of the null point need concern us because any other possible agreement would be vetoed by one or both of the players.

Now suppose Andrew and Doris each demand a payoff halfway between their best outcome (at H) and their worst (at the origin). Then relative to Orville's and Frances' best and worst outcomes, it costs Orville more to meet this demand than it costs Frances.   This is because the solid line is lower than the dotted line in the range

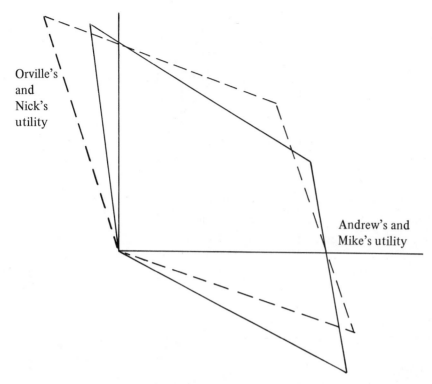

Orville's
and
Nick's
utility

Andrew's and
Mike's utility

FIGURE 2.5. Two Normalized Games That Are Hard to Compare

between 0 and 1.   Indeed, no matter what demand is made, it costs Orville more than it costs Frances to give in.   To turn the situation around, it costs Andrew more to give in to any demand by Orville than it costs Doris to give in to an equivalent demand by Frances.   So Andrew and Orville certainly have more conflict of interest than do Doris and Frances.

Empiricist: But often this kind of comparison is impossible.   You can't make such an easy comparison between the game between Mike and Nick (dotted lines in Figure 2-5) and the old game between Andrew and Orville.   For equal demands by Andrew and Mike it might cost Orville more than it costs Nick to give in, or it might cost Orville less.   It depends on which demand is made.

Theoretician: Quite right.   The concept of cost of meeting a demand is not by itself sufficient to tell us which of these two games has more conflict of interest, since for some demands the cost in one game is higher and for other demands the cost in the other game is

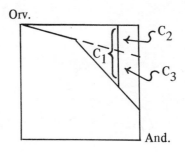

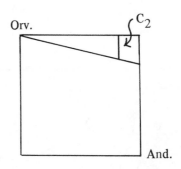

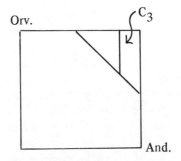

FIGURE 2-6. Three Games to
Illustrate Additivity

higher. Incidentally, this is also the limitation of concepts like Pruit's ease of generosity and its inverse, Boulding's coefficient of conflict.

So let's take a different tack. Suppose we have three games between Andrew and Orville (Figure 2-6) which are related to each other in a very simple way: in the first game the cost (C_1) to Orville of meeting a demand by Andrew is the sum of the costs ($C_2 + C_3$)

to Orville in the other two games for meeting the same demand.   Then what would you say about the conflicts of interest in these three games?

Empiricist: Obviously the conflict of interest of the first game is greater than that of either of the other two.   I can go further though. Without even knowing which demand Andrew is making I can say that the cost of meeting it in the first game will be equal to the sum of the costs of meeting it in the other two games.   So it seems reasonable that the first game should have exactly as much conflict of interest as the other two put together.

Theoretician: That's what I was hoping you would say, and I agree.   In fact, it is just this which I had in mind for the last property, called *additivity*.   In normalized games, if the cost to one player of meeting a demand by the other is the sum of the costs of meeting the same demand in two other games, then the conflict of interest of that game is the sum of the conflicts of interest of the other two games.

Empiricist: But what if the roles are interchanged so that Andrew is considering meeting a demand by Orville?

Theoretician: That's no problem for the analysis because the property of symmetry already guarantees that it won't make any difference for the measurement of conflict of interest if we interchange the roles of the players.

Empiricist: That takes care of the problem of who makes the demand and who responds.   But additivity still applies only in a very special case.

Theoretician: That's right.   It holds only if the games are already normalized and if the costs of meeting a demand sum correctly no matter which demand is made.

Empiricist: Then I don't see how it can be used to compare games like the ones in Figure 5, where the costs of meeting some demands are higher in one game and the costs of meeting other demands are higher in the other game.

Theoretician: Used by itself it can't, even though it is the most powerful of the properties.

C. Proof of the Existence and Uniqueness of the Definition

Empiricist: You promised before that when I agreed to a list of properties that must be satisfied by the procedure to measure conflict of interest in bargaining games, there would be one and only one procedure that worked.   I've agreed to symmetry, independence, continuity, boundedness, and additivity.   Is this the list you had in mind?

Theoretician: Yes, just those five.

TABLE 2-4

Properties which should be satisfied by any procedure to measure conflict of interest in bargaining games:

1. *Symmetry:* invariance with respect to interchange of the labels of the players.
2. *Independence:* independence with respect to choice of representation of players' utility schedules.
3. *Continuity:* for a given game, G, and an infinite sequence of games, G_i, all with the same no agreement point, if the region of G is the limit of the regions of G_i then the conflict of interest of G is the limit of the conflicts of interest of the games G_i.
4. *Boundedness:* the bargaining game with the most conflict of interest has conflict of interest equal to $\frac{1}{2}$.
5. *Additivity:* in normalized games, if the cost to one player of meeting a demand by the other is the sum of the costs of meeting the same demand in the two other games, then the conflict of interest of that game is the sum of the conflicts of interest of the other two games.

The Procedure: normalize the game, and calculate the area in the unit square which lies above and to the right of the region of feasible outcomes.

Theorem: 1. The procedure satisfies the five properties.
2. There is no other way to satisfy them.

Empiricist: Well, then, what is the one procedure that works?

Theoretician: Just this: normalize the game and calculate the area in the unit square which lies above and to the right of the region of feasible outcomes (see Figures 2-7 and 2-8 for examples). That is the conflict of interest in the bargaining game. The proof that this scheme works is almost trivial. The proof that it is the only scheme that works is not as easy, but it is quite straightforward.

Empiricist: First let me make sure this scheme satisfies each of the five properties. I can do most of the proof myself. The procedure certainly satisfies symmetry because the area is the same if I put Andrew on the vertical axis and Orville on the horizontal axis (Figure 2-9). I can also see that it is independent of which way I originally represented the utility schedules because the measurement of the area is done only after the game is normalized. Continuity is easy because if one of the points were moved a little bit then the area would change only a little bit. That leaves boundedness and additivity. Let's take boundedness first. Why is $\frac{1}{2}$ the most conflict of interest a bargaining game can have?

Theoretician: Remember that in measuring the area we are using the normalized version of the game. This means that the no agreement point is at the origin and the best each player can do is set equal

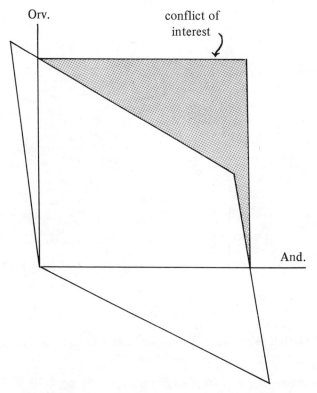

FIGURE 2-7.   Normalized Apple-Orange Game

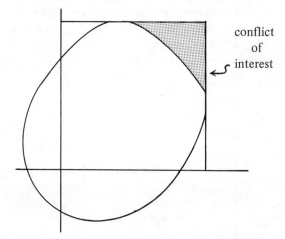

FIGURE 2-8.   Another Normalized Bargaining
Game

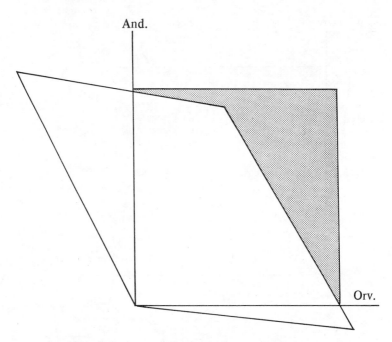

FIGURE 2-9.   Interchange of Labels of the Players in
Apple-Orange Game

to 1.   Therefore some point along line a in Figure 2-10 is feasible
and some point along line b must also be feasible.   Since these two
points are feasible, any point on a straight line between them is also
feasible by means of randomization between these two points (see Figure 2-11).   The area above and to the right of this straight line is
the maximum conflict of interest the game can have given that these
two points are feasible.   The largest this area can be is one half of the

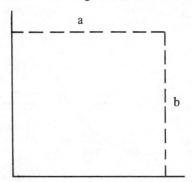

FIGURE 2-10.   The Unit Square

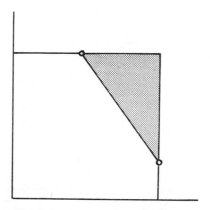

FIGURE 2-11. Maximum Conflict
of Interest for These Two Feasible
Agreements

unit square.   Hence the amount of conflict of interest cannot exceed ½.

Empiricist: Now I see why you wanted to make ½ the upper
bound on conflict of interest in bargaining games.   It lets us use the
area beyond the region of feasible agreements to measure the amount
of conflict of interest in a game.   If you had followed my suggestion
to make 1 the upper bound we would always have to mutiply this
area by 2 to get the conflict of interest in a game.

Theoretician: Right.   Now there is only one more property to
verify, and that is additivity.   Take another look at Figure 2-6, and
recall that for any demand Andrew makes (that is, for any point on
the horizontal axis) the cost to Orville of meeting this demand in the
first game is the sum of the costs in the other two games.   This means
that the height of the area we are using to measure conflict of interest
must be the same in the first game as the sum of the heights in the
other two.   If this holds for every one of Andrew's demands (which
means every point on the horizontal axis), then the areas themselves
must sum.   Therefore the conflict of interest areas add up correctly
in the three games if the costs of meeting any demand add up.   This
of course is exactly what the property of additivity requires.

Now you have seen that my procedure to measure conflict of
interest satisfies symmetry, independence, continuity, boundedness, and
additivity.

Empiricist: But why couldn't someone else discover another
scheme that also worked?   For that matter, how do you know I don't
have another procedure in mind that satisfies the five properties?

Theoretician: Let's suppose you do.   I'm going to show you that

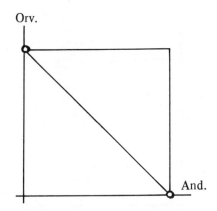

FIGURE 2-12.   Nut-Bolt Game

for any bargaining game at all your procedure must give the same answer as the procedure I proposed.   In that case, your precedure is identical to mine, and there is only one way to measure conflict of interest in bargaining games which satisfies the five properties.

First, I'll show you that we get the same answer for the game in Figure 2-12.   An example of a game that has a graph of this form is one in which Andrew has a nut and Orville has a bolt, and neither player can derive any use from the other's piece unless he has them both.

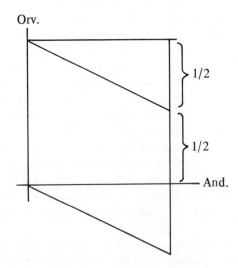

FIGURE 2-13.   Andrew Cares Only
for Orange

Empiricist: I know your procedure gives an answer of ½ because that is the area beyond the region of feasible agreements, but how do you know my scheme gives the same answer?

Theoretician: Your scheme cannot give any other game a higher conflict of interest because it has to satisfy additivity.   Since it is impossible to make it any harder for one side to meet the demands of the other side, it is impossible to add any conflict of interest to this game. Once I know that your procedure gives maximum conflict of interest to this game, I also know that it gives it exactly ½ because your scheme must also satisfy boundedness.   So we agree on the first game.

Now I can tell you how much conflict of interest your procedure must give for the game in Figure 2-13.   This might be the game in which Andrew has an apple and Orville has an orange, but Andrew cares only about the orange while Orville values the apple halfway between the orange and both pieces of fruit.   For any demand Andrew makes in this game (relative to his best and worst outcomes, of course) the cost to Orville of meeting it is exactly one half of the cost of meeting the same demand in the nut-bolt game.   Therefore since your scheme satisfies additivity, it must give two of these games as much conflict of interest as the nut-bolt game.   I already know that your scheme gives the nut-bolt game a conflict of interest of ½, so it must give the game in Figure 2-13 a conflict of interest of ¼.

Now let's change the game so Orville regards the apple as ¾ of the way from an orange to both, while Andrew still does not care about his apple (Figure 2-14a).

Empiricist: I see what you are driving at.   Two games such as

Orv.

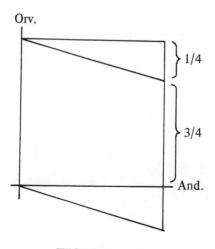

FIGURE 2-14a

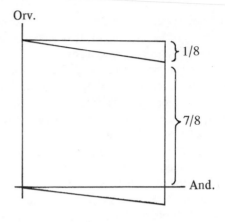

FIGURE 2-14b

these must have the same amount of conflict of interest as the previous game, so each must have a conflict of interest of ⅛.

Theoretician: And if Orville regards the apple as ⅞ of the way from an orange to both (Figure 2-14b)?

Empiricist: Then my scheme must give it half of the previous game, or ¹⁄₁₆.

Theoretician: And if Orville regards the apple as ⅝ of the way from an orange to both (Figure 2-14c)?

Empiricist: Then the conflict of interest of the game in which the apple was ¾ of the way for Orville (Figure 2-14a), plus the conflict of

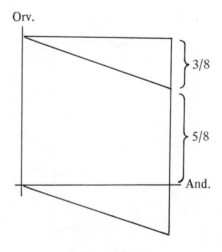

FIGURE 2-14c

Orv.

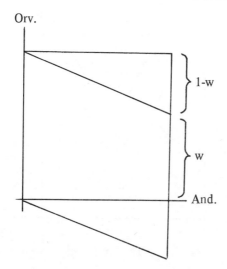

FIGURE 2-15.   Andrew Cares Only
for Orange: General Form

interest of the game in which the apple was $\frac{7}{8}$ of the way for Orville (Figure 2-14b), must be the conflict of interest of this game.   So if Orville regards the apple as $\frac{5}{8}$ of the way from an orange to both the conflict of interest is $\frac{3}{16}$.

Theoretician: Right.   Any procedure to measure conflict of interest which satisfies the five properties must give a value of $\frac{3}{16}$ for the game in Figure 2-14c.   And in general, if the apple were m/n of the way, we could add the costs of meeting a demand in $n - m$ games in which the apple were $1 - 1/n$ of the way.   Each of these games would have a conflict of interest of $\frac{1}{2}(1/n)$, so the total conflict of interest would be $\frac{1}{2}((n-m)/n)$ or $\frac{1}{2}(1 - m/n)$.

Empiricist: What if the value of the apple to Orville were not an exact fraction?   Say it was w.   (Figure 2-15)

Theoretician: Then I could find some fractions that were closer and closer approximations to w, and I could devise a sequence of games using these fractions.   This sequence of games would have their regions become closer and closer approximations of the region of the game with w.   Your scheme satisfies continuity so I know that the limit of the conflicts of interest of these games must equal the conflict of interest of the game in Figure 2-15.   I also know that the conflicts of interest of the games with the fractions must get closer and closer to $\frac{1}{2}(1 - w)$ since the fractions themselves get closer and closer to w.

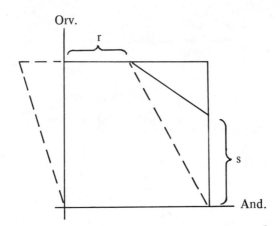

FIGURE 2-16.   A Money Game

Therefore this must also be the conflict of interest of the game in Figure 2-15.

So far I have discussed only simple trading games. Now let's take a look at a slightly more general case of the bargaining game such as the one shown with solid lines in Figure 2-16. A simple example of this kind of game is one in which two players are offered $1.50 if they can agree on how to split it up, and are limited to no more than $1.00 each. I am also assuming for the sake of simplicity that the players are indifferent between a given amount of money and an even chance of getting twice as much. In this simple example, $r = \frac{1}{2}$ and $s = \frac{1}{2}$.

Your procedure must say that the conflict of interest of this game is $(1 - s)$ times the conflict of interest of the game shown in dotted lines. This is so by the reasoning we have just used on the game in Figure 2-15. But the game with the dotted lines is just the game we saw before in Figure 2-15 provided that $w = r$ and the players are interchanged. But since your procedure must satisfy symmetry, interchanging the labels of the players makes no difference, so the dotted game in Figure 2-16 must have the same conflict as the game in Figure 2-15, namely $\frac{1}{2}(1 - r)$. As I said before, the solid game has $(1 - s)$ times the conflict of interest of the dotted game. Therefore your procedure must give the solid game in Figure 2-16 a conflict of interest of $\frac{1}{2}(1 - r)(1 - s)$. This is also the size of the area beyond the region of feasible agreements so our two schemes give the same result for this kind of game too.

Empiricist: What about a more complex game like the one in Figure

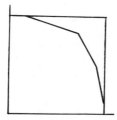

FIGURE 2-17.
A Kinked Game

2-17? How can you be sure that my procedure gives the same answer as yours?

Theoretician: Take a look at the three games in Figures 2-18a, 2-18b, and 2-18c. These are constructed so that the costs to Orville of meeting one of Andrew's demands add up to the cost of meeting the same demand in game 2-17. The game in Figure 2-18d is constructed so that the costs are the sum of the costs of two games in Figures 2-18a and 2-18b. I know that your scheme gives the same answer as mine for each of the games in Figure 2-18a and 2-18b, so by additivity I know that it gives the same answer for the game in Figure 2-18d, which is the sum of the ones in 2-18a and 2-18b. The game in Figure 2-17 must have the same amount of conflict of interest as the sum of the conflicts of interest of the game in Figure 2-18c and the game in Figure 2-18d again by additivity. Therefore I know that our two schemes give the same answer for the conflict of interest of the kinked game in Figure 2-17. And this reasoning applies no matter how many kinks there are.

Empiricist: What about a game like the one in Figure 2-19 in which Orville's most preferred outcome would give Andrew more than his no agreement value?

Theoretician: Well, if Andrew's demand is low enough, Orville can meet it at no cost whatever. So the game has the same conflict of interest as the one in Figure 2-20 since one consequence of additivity is that two games with the same costs of meeting each demand must have the same conflict of interest.

Empiricist: And the game in Figure 2-20 is just like the one in Figure 2-17, so we know how to handle it. What if the normalized game has a region of feasible agreements with smooth boundary like the one in Figure 2-21?

Theoretician: That's easy too. After all, I can draw a sequence of games with kinked boundaries like the one in Figure 2-17. By using more and more kinks I can ensure that the regions of this se-

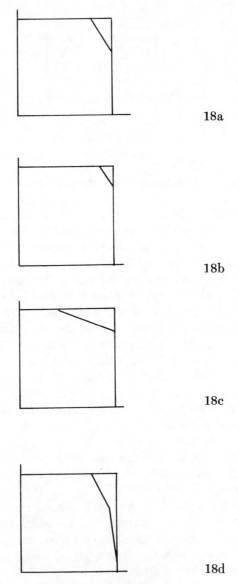

18a

18b

18c

18d

FIGURE 2-18. How to
Calculate Conflict of In-
terest of the Kinked
Game

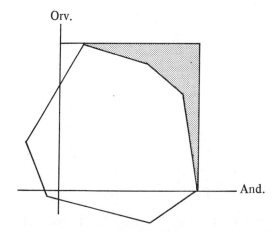

FIGURE 2-19.   Andrew's Worst Isn't Orville's
Best

quence of games will be closer and closer approximations of the region of the smooth game in Figure 2-21.   I already know that your scheme gives the same answer as mine for each of the kinked games in the sequence, so it must give the same for the limit of these games.   Since both our procedures satisfy continuity, each of their limits must be the value of the smooth game.   But both our procedures give the same answer for the limit, so both must give the same answer for the conflict of interest of the smooth game.

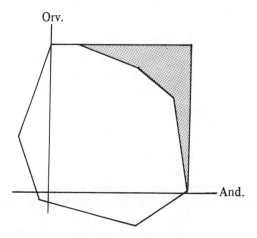

FIGURE 2-20.   Game with Same Conflict
of Interest As Previous One

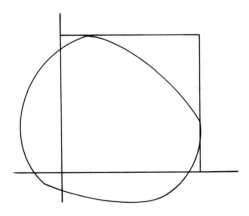

FIGURE 2-21.   A Bargaining Game with
Smooth Boundary

Empiricist: What if the game I pick is not normalized?

Theoretician: Then I can redraw the game in normalized form by selecting a new representation of the utility schedules of the players. This won't affect the answer our schemes give because both have the property of independence with respect to this kind of change.   Therefore, since our two procedures give the same result for all normalized games, they give the same result for all unnormalized games as well.

Empiricist: I've run out of types of games.

Theoretician: Exactly.   Whatever scheme you might devise which satisfies symmetry, independence, boundedness, continuity, and additivity must give the same conflict of interest as the procedure I proposed.   And they must give the same result for every possible bargaining game.   Therefore they are actually identical ways to measure conflict of interest in bargaining games, and are not really different schemes after all.   So if you want to know how much conflict of interest a bargaining game has, first normalize it and then calculate the area in the unit square which lies above and to the right of the region of feasible agreements.

D. Intuitive Justification

Empiricist: I realize your procedure works in the sense that it satisfies the five properties we agreed to, but what if we forget about these properties?   Does the procedure still make sense?

Theoretician: Sure it does.   Notice that the more the region of feasible agreements bulges within the unit square, the less conflict of interest there is.   The intuitive justification that this is indeed the correct way to measure conflict of interest in bargaining games is simply that the more the region bulges outward, the better both players can simultaneously do, and hence the less incompatible are the goals of the players. For example, if the region bulges a great deal, the players can both get nearly their best payoff, so their conflict of interest is low.

Another way to look at it is to see that each player's reasonable demands are between his best and worst outcomes. The joint demand area is the rectangle which becomes the unit square when the game is normalized. Normalized or not, conflict of interest is simply the proportion of the joint demand area which is infeasible. This proportion does not change when the representation of the utility schedules changes, so normalization is not even necessary to measure conflict of interest (see Figure 2-22) with this alternate procedure which is equivalent to the original procedure.

Empiricist: That's neat, but isn't the procedure too sensitive to what a player's best and worst outcomes are? After all, if one of these points changes, the size of the joint demand area changes.

Theoretician: That's right, but so does the size of the region of feasible agreements. The net result is what you would want it to be. What you have to consider is not just the size of the joint demand area, but the proportion of that area which is infeasible.

Empiricist: But can you tell me why that is a good way to measure conflict of interest?

Theoretician: Sure. Look at it this way. The lower the proportion of the joint demand area which is infeasible, the less incompatible are the goals of the players. In an extreme case, none of the joint

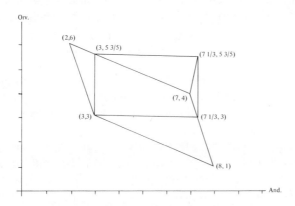

FIGURE 2-22.   How to Calculate Conflict of
Interest in Apple-Orange Game

demand area is infeasible, so both players can get their maximum demands at once and there is no conflict of interest between them.   As the proportion of the joint demand area which is infeasible increases, the players are no longer able to do as well simultaneously, and the conflict of interest between them increases.   The larger the proportion of the joint demand area which is infeasible, the greater is the conflict of interest.   In fact, the proposed procedure to measure conflict of interest in a bargaining game is just to calculate this proportion.   So the procedure is justifiable even without reference to the five properties.

The best way to understand the meaning of this procedure to measure conflict of interest is to use it.   The original game between Andrew and Orville is repeated in Figure 2-22.   The rectangle represents the joint demand area and has dimensions of $4\frac{1}{3}$ by $2\frac{3}{5}$.   Therefore the joint demand area is the product of these two dimensions, namely $\frac{169}{15}$. The area within this rectangle which is infeasible can easily be divided into two triangles.   The upper one has an area of $\frac{1}{2}(4\frac{1}{3})(1\frac{3}{5}) = \frac{104}{30}$.   The area of the lower one is $\frac{1}{2}(\frac{1}{3})(2\frac{3}{5}) = \frac{13}{30}$.   The sum of the areas of the two triangles is $\frac{104}{30} + \frac{13}{30} = \frac{117}{30}$.   Therefore the proportion of the joint demand area which is infeasible is $(\frac{117}{30})/(\frac{169}{15}) = \frac{117}{338} = .35$.   If the game were first normalized, the area within the unit square beyond the region of feasible agreements would also be .35.

The exact amount of conflict of interest in any bargaining game can be calculated just by taking the ratio of two areas.   So the first achievement of the procedure is to allow the comparison of *any* two bargaining games to see which has greater conflict of interest.   This means that if you have any hypotheses about how conflict of interest affects behavior you can now test them because I can tell you how much conflict of interest there is in each of your bargaining games.

E. Altering Conflict of Interest

Practical Man: So what?   I'm not interested in studying politics, I'm interested in practicing politics.   What have you got for me?

Theoretician: How would you like to know how to lower conflict of interest?

Practical Man: Sure.   But before you go on, let me point out that sometimes I might want more rather than less conflict of interest. For example, Martin Luther King made the distinction between a negative peace, which is the absence of tension, and a positive peace, which is the presence of justice.   He said in 1963 that the purpose of nonviolent direct action was to create such a crisis and such creative tension that a community had to confront the issue.   And remember that the authors of the Constitution deliberately arranged for there to be conflict of interest between the President and Congress, and between the House of Representatives and the Senate.   So I'm not very satisfied with the kind of unequivocal denunciation of conflict of interest and conflictful behavior so often heard.

Theoretician: That's interesting, but it certainly doesn't create any theoretical difficulties.   If the theory can tell us how to lower conflict of interest, it can also tell us how to raise it.   I'll leave it to you to decide which is appropriate to do in a given circumstance.

Practical Man: I still don't need your theory.   I already know what is needed to raise or lower conflict of interest.   I may not be able to express it in the formal terms you like to use, but common sense is all I need.

Theoretician: What do you have in mind?

Practical Man: I like to think in terms of a specific example.   Let's see—how about the recent reapportionment problem in Connecticut which arose when the courts ordered the state legislature reapportioned?   The Democrats and Republicans had to bargain with each other in a Constitutional Convention to determine what the new boundaries of the districts would be.

Theoretician: What would have happened if they hadn't reached an agreement?

Practical Man: Well, the court set a deadline and threatened to have the Yale Computer Center redistrict the state if the deadline was not met.

Theoretician: I bet the party leaders didn't like that idea at all.

Practical Man: I should think not, but their only other choice was to come to an agreement, which they managed to do less than two weeks before the deadline.

Theoretician: This looks like a nice two-person bargaining game. The Democrats and Republicans were probably cohesive enough to be regarded as the participants, and the court refused to negotiate.

Practical Man: Right.   There may have been a lot of bargaining within the parties, too, but let's just worry about the bargaining between them since this was such a partisan issue.   The parties could, in effect, make binding agreements because they had no way to double-cross each other.   Any failure to support an agreement would just leave the parties in a deadlock and they would still face the court's threat.   A few mavericks would not have prevented the parties from passing any-thing they agreed on.

Theoretician: The court threat was the no agreement point.   No one knew what that outcome would mean, but since parties couldn't have any influence on it, the threat could be regarded as fixed for them.   Its utility for each participant could be determined by asking them to compare it to specific reapportionment plans.

Practical Man: And we can assume that almost any plan which was proposed by both parties and approved by the court would be acceptable to the voters.

Theoretician: Now, you said that you already knew what would be needed to raise or lower conflict of interest.   What do you have in mind for this example?

Practical Man: Well, to start with, I would say that if someone constructed a new plan in which the parties were interested, this would certainly lower the conflict of interest.

Theoretician: You mean that if someone discovered a new way to expand outward the region of feasible agreements the conflict of interest would be lowered.   (Figure 2-23, points A and B)

Practical Man: Yes, provided of course that the new possibilities were advantageous to both players.

Theoretician: By advantageous you mean that the new possibilities lie above and to the right of the old region, I take it.

Practical Man: Correct, but also that they must be preferred by both sides to the no agreement point.   Otherwise they would never be chosen.

Theoretician: Very good.   So if points such as A and B could be added to the game in Figure 2-23 this would necessarily reduce the conflict of interest?

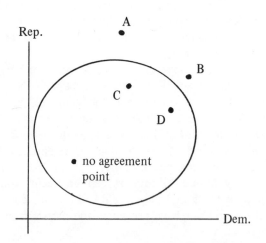

FIGURE 2-23.   Reapportionment Game

Practical Man: Right. Now I have another idea, one that is related to the previous thought. If some outcomes that were feasible agreements are eliminated then the conflict of interest is obviously increased. Again, I'm assuming these are ones that might actually have been settled upon. In other words they are points like C and D in Figure 2-23 which are preferred by both players to the no agreement point.

Theoretician: I take it you aren't really talking about the elimination of a single agreement, but the actual shrinkage of the size of the region of feasible agreements.

Practical Man: Good point. It wouldn't make much difference if one possible agreement were eliminated while others that were practically identical remained. I mean that the conflict of interest would be increased if the region actually shrank.

Theoretician: That gives us two principles to think about. You've talked about changing the region of feasible agreements. Can you say anything about the no agreement point? What if the court increased its threat, say by specifying that its own plan would definitely not take into account the current bailiwicks of the incumbents?

Practical Man: I guess that wouldn't help them any because even after negotiation they might not reach an agreement. So it would increase the potential stakes of the bargaining and might increase the antagonisms. I guess it might well increase the conflict of interest.

Theoretician: Anything else?

Practical Man: Here's another principle: It's clear that if people don't understand each other's preferences things can only be worse than if they do. So a full and accurate understanding of each other and the situation can only help to reduce conflict of interest.

Theoretician: Let me ask about one more point to see if we can develop a fifth principle. In game theory there is something called a side payment, which is simply a commodity that can be transferred from one player to another, is available in any desired amount, and is linear in utility for both players. By linear in utility I mean that a player is indifferent between a certain amount and an even chance of twice as much. Often pennies are assumed to have these characteristics in laboratory gaming. When side payments are available, the players can settle on a feasible agreement and make a side payment from one to the other. This allows them to add some new possibilities to the region of feasible outcomes.

Practical Man: That's a pretty restrictive definition. It rules out a lot of what is commonly thought of as side payments in politics. But even in your restricted use of the term, using side payments is a fairly common practice in bargaining even when money doesn't change hands.

Theoretician: When side payments are possible, does it affect the conflict of interest?

Practical Man: Sure.   It ought to lower it because it adds a whole range of new possibilities that may be just what is needed to reach an agreement.

Theoretician: Now we have five interesting principles to guide us in practical action.

Practical Man: Right, and they all come from common sense thinking.   I didn't need your formal scheme, did I?

Theoretician: I have a surprise for you.   I think each one of your five common sense principles is wrong.   And I think I can get you to agree with me.   First, you said that if new feasible agreements could be added that were preferred by both players to the no agreement point then conflict of interest would necessarily fall.   To return to the reappportionment example, let's suppose the Republicans discovered a new way of districting the state which they preferred over any other plan, and one which was still better for the Democrats than a court-ordered reapportionment.   Point A in Figure 2-24 represents such a plan.   Once it is discovered, the game is transformed into the one in Figure 2-25 because all intermediate outcomes are assumed feasible, if only by randomizations.   Now the new game (Figure 2-25) actually has more conflict of interest than the old one because the proportion of the joint demand area which is infeasible has increased. The region of feasible agreements has certainly increased, but the joint

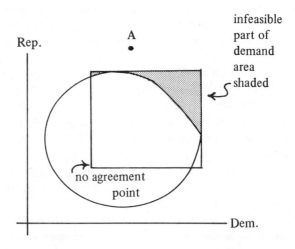

FIGURE 2-24.   Before Discovery of Plan A

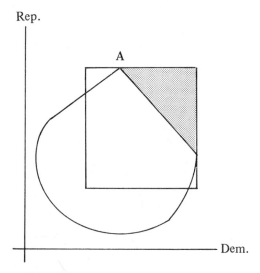

Rep.

A

Dem.

FIGURE 2-25.   After Discovery of Plan A

demand area has increased even more because the new point greatly increased the best hope of one of the players.

Practical Man: Still, the players might prefer the new situation to the old.

Theoretician: Yes, they might, but only because they might both benefit, not because the conflict of interest is lower.   Before the discovery of point A the best hopes of both sides were relatively modest, and there were feasible compromise agreements that gave both sides a high proportion of what they could hope for.   But with the discovery of point A, the best hopes of the Republicans increased a great deal. Yet, none of the compromise agreements that also became available could provide both sides with as high a proportion of their best hopes as before.   Thus agreement could be expected to be more difficult.   Or to put it another way, conflict of interest increased.   This is illustrated in Figure 2-25 where the region of feasible agreements does not bulge as much as it did in Figure 2-24.   So the discovery of point A actually increased the conflict of interest.   Of course, if we wanted to know exactly how much the conflict of interest went up we could calculate the proportions of the joint demand areas which are infeasible in Figure 2-24 and 2-25.

Practical Man: My second principle assumed that making the region smaller has to raise the conflict of interest and was based on similar reasoning, so I guess it is wrong too.

Rep.

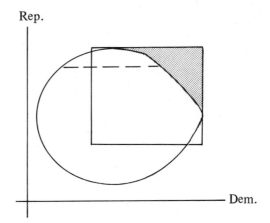

FIGURE 2-26.   Before Republicans
Hopes Lowered

Theoretician: Yes, and it's wrong for similar reasons.   Suppose the court ruled that the most preferred plans of one or both parties were unacceptable.   Figures 2-26 and 2-27 show what would happen if this was done to the Republicans.   Clearly, the elimination of the possibility of making these high demands makes it possible for both sides simultaneously to do nearly as well as they could possibly hope. So the conflict of interest is decreased.

Practical Man: Now I'm not so sure of the third point: if the

Rep.

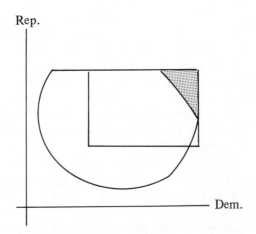

FIGURE 2-27.   After Republican
Hopes Lowered

Rep.

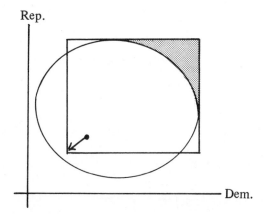

Dem.

FIGURE 2-28.   Increased Threat

no agreement point is made less desirable the conflict of interest has to increase.   If the court increased its threat (Figure 2-28) the relative bulge of the region would also increase, so the conflict of interest would be reduced.

Theoretician: You're catching on.   The idea here is that lowering the no agreement point will always increase the demand area, but it will also increase the range of feasible agreements at least at the same rate.   Therefore conflict of interest is decreased as the proportion of the demand area which is infeasible decreases.

Practical Man: What about the idea that misunderstanding can only raise the conflict of interest?

Theoretician: A look at Figures 2-29 and 2-30 will show you

Rep.

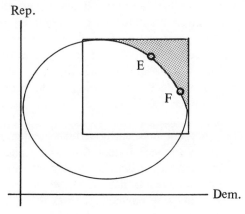

Dem.

FIGURE 2-29.   Actual Situation

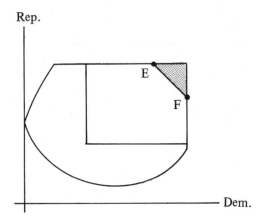

FIGURE 2-30.   If the Parties Perceive
Tough Court

that this is not necessarily so.   Suppose the true region of feasible
agreements is the one shown in Figure 2-29, but the players both (mis-
takenly) believe the court will not accept those plans that are very
favorable to either party.   Then they think the game they are playing
looks like the one in Figure 2-30.   They will negotiate as if there
were little conflict of interest and they are quite likely to have little
trouble agreeing on some point between E and F.   Moreover, if they
do, they will get the payoffs they expected, and be none the wiser.
Their misperceptions may actually help them.   One thing is clear
though: behavior depends on beliefs about the consequences of acts
rather than the actual consequences.   If the players perceive a game
with low conflict of interest they will behave accordingly.   In a real
sense, a game has low conflict of interest if the players think it does.

Practical Man: I guess I was too hasty.   Some types of misunderstanding can lower the perceived conflict of interest and thereby make
agreements easier.   I certainly would not go so far as to say that misunderstanding is always a valuable thing though.

Theoretician: Nor would I.   That brings us to your last principle,
that side payments reduce the conflict of interest by expanding the
region of feasible agreements.   We have already agreed than an expansion of the region does not necessarily reduce conflict of interest, so
now there is no reason to believe that this is the effect of allowing
side payments.   Actually side payments will make the boundary of
the region of feasible agreements flat, as shown in Figures 2-31 and
2-32.   Therefore allowing side payments causes the conflict of interest
to be $\frac{1}{2}$ no matter what the original game was like.

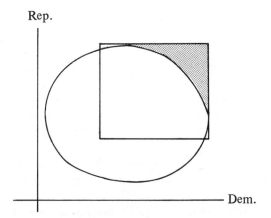

FIGURE 2-31.   If Side Payments
Not Allowed

If you want to know how to change the conflict of interest in a bargaining game, a few correct guidelines are easy enough to supply. To check their validity simply see what the change in a game does to the proportion of the joint demand area which is infeasible.   Don't forget that the demand area itself might be changed by a change in the game.

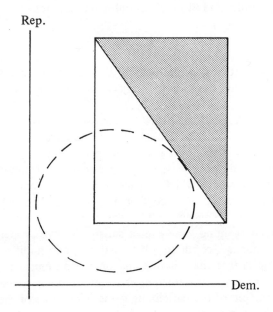

FIGURE 2-32.   If Side Payments Allowed

Here are correct versions of the five principles we've just been examining:

1. An expansion of the region of feasible agreements will lower conflict of interest provided that the maximum either player can hope to achieve is not raised. An expansion can take place by the addition of new feasible outcomes (perhaps by realization of their prior existence or by technical advances) or by the re-evaluation of the utility of old feasible outcomes (perhaps through persuasion).
2. A contraction of the region of feasible outcomes due to foreclosure of the demands of one or both players above a certain level will lower conflict of interest.
3. A lowering of the utility of the no agreement point for one or both players cannot increase the conflict of interest and in most cases will reduce it.
4. Misunderstanding can either raise or lower the amount of conflict of interest perceived by the players. The three points above show how this can happen. For example, if the players think the no agreement point will bring worse results than it actually will, they will perceive a lower conflict of interest.
5. Allowing side payments gives the bargaining game maximum conflict of interest. This is true because side payments are, by definition, linear in utility and available in unlimited amounts.

F. Summary

Empiricist: It would be helpful if you would summarize what you've said about the whole subject of conflict of interest and bargaining.

Theoretician: Glad to. First of all, we've seen that some of the basic strategic problems of bargaining are captured in the bargaining game invented by Nash. In games of this type two players can talk to each other and make a binding agreement, but there is a single predetermined outcome which occurs if no agreement is reached.

Then we discussed what conflict of interest in this type of interaction should mean. You agreed that any procedure to measure conflict of interest in bargaining games must satisfy the five properties of symmetry, independence, continuity, boundedness, and additivity. The interesting thing is that there is one and only one definition that satisfies all these properties. This definition is that conflict of interest in the normalized version of the bargaining game is the area of the unit square which lies above and to the right of the region of feasible agreements.

An alternative way of stating this definition is the proportion of the joint demand area which is infeasible. We proved that this definition satisfies the five properties, and that any other scheme which also satisfies them gives the same answer for any given bargaining game and is therefore really the same definition of conflict of interest.

Not only is this the only adequate definition in terms of the five properties, but it also makes sense intuitively. This is because the less incompatible are the goals of the players, the more the region of feasible agreements bulges and thus the less conflict of interest there is.

Finally, I showed the Practical Man that many of his ideas on how conflict of interest could be altered were not always correct. His problem was that without a formal definition he didn't have a clear idea how to employ the concept. Then I used my definition to derive a number of results which can guide him if he wants to change the conflict of interest in an actual situation.

3

Conflict of Interest
and the Dilemma
of Collective Action

A. The Nature of the Problem

THE PRISONER'S DILEMMA

In many political situations the participants are not able to make
binding agreements, and hence cooperation between them cannot rest
on a sure foundation.   The idea of conflict of interest is still applicable
since the extent to which the players' goals are incompatible will still
help determine how they will choose to act.   The basic theme is again
that the more conflict of interest there is, the more likely it is that
the players will act conflictfully.

The bargaining game examined in the previous chapter does not
exhaust the strategic issues involved even in a simple exchange of an
apple and an orange.   Among non-zero-sum games a distinction is
made between those which allow communication and binding agreements and those which do not.   Games which do are called cooperative

games, but this terminology should not be taken as necessarily implying anything about the amount of conflict of interest in such games.   The bargaining game is a particular kind of cooperative game whose distinctive aspect is that while the players can make a binding agreement on any one of a variety of outcomes, there is a single predetermined outcome which occurs if no agreement is reached.

This chapter examines the meaning of conflict of interest in the context of the most famous kind of noncooperative game, the Prisoner's Dilemma.   The fascination of the Prisoner's Dilemma is that in this game two individuals pursuing their individual gain will not achieve the common good and therefore both will suffer.

An example of the Prisoner's Dilemma is provided by forbidding communication and binding agreements in a simple bargaining game. The original game between Andrew and Orville will do nicely.   Recall that Andrew has an apple and Orville has an orange but each prefers the other's fruit.   Playing a bargaining game, Andrew and Orville can discuss the various possible trades (including randomizations between elementary trades), and try to agree on a feasible outcome.   But, playing a Prisoner's Dilemma, they are not allowed to talk to each other.   Each must independently decide what to do with his own piece of fruit.   Andrew can either keep his apple or give it to Orville, but he must decide without knowing for sure what Orville will do.   Likewise Orville does not know what Andrew will do, and can either keep his orange or give it away.   The game is represented in the payoff matrix below, using the original utility schedules from Table 2-1 of the previous chapter.   The first number in each cell is the payoff to Andrew (the row chooser) and the second is the payoff to Orville (the column chooser).

What should rational players do?   The answer is quite simple: each should keep his own fruit no matter what he thinks the other

TABLE 3-1
A Prisoner's Dilemma

| | | Orville | |
		Keep Orange	Give Orange to Andrew
	Keep Apple	3,3	8,1
Andrew	Give Apple to Orville	2,6	7,4

will do.   Without the ability to communicate and reach binding agreements, giving something away only lowers a player's utility without increasing the likelihood of receiving something in return.   So Andrew should keep his apple and Orville should keep his orange.   This is only rational.   But both players could have done better had each given away their own piece of fruit.   Andrew would then have had the orange he preferred, and Orville would have had the apple he preferred.   This then is the dilemma: each player can individually do better by keeping his fruit, but they can both do better by giving their fruit away.

This is also the dilemma of collective action.   Two or more individuals pursuing their own interests may not achieve their common interests.   This theme has been one of the major concerns among political commentators from Hobbes, Locke, and Rousseau to Olson (1965).   Specific political applications of the dilemma of collective action and its resolution are discussed in Part II.   This chapter will examine the meaning of conflict of interest in situations of this type, make predictions about how people behave when faced with the Prisoner's Dilemma, and test these predictions with data from laboratory experiments.

CONFLICT OF INTEREST IN THE PRISONER'S DILEMMA

There is certainly some conflict of interest in the sample Prisoner's Dilemma between Andrew and Orville, but it is not unlimited.   The players have a common interest in achieving an exchange, even though they cannot bind each other to a promise to give up their own fruit to get the other one.   Of course their interests also diverge since each also wishes to keep his own fruit.   Not only are there common and conflicting interests in a Prisoner's Dilemma, but some Prisoner's Dilemmas have more or less conflict of interest than do others.   The less each player cares about his own fruit, for example, the less conflict of interest there is.

Of course, a narrowly rational person who is playing a Prisoner's Dilemma game just once will not give anything away no matter how little or how much conflict of interest there is.   However, if the game is played more than once, the strategic situation changes.   There is now good reason to establish a record of cooperation to encourage the other player to cooperate.   Even so, there are still reasons not to cooperate, including immediate gains and a desire to teach the other player a lesson if he has not been cooperating.   In different Prisoner's Dilemma games these different kinds of incentives have different strengths, making mutual cooperation more or less difficult to achieve.

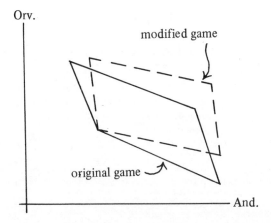

FIGURE 3-1.   Two Prisoner's Dilemmas—
Easy Comparison

Conflict of interest measures this difficulty.   To put it another way, conflict of interest in a Prisoner's Dilemma measures what Rapoport and Chammah (1965, 35) call how "mild" or "severe" the game is.

Looking at specific Prisoner's Dilemma games will help formalize this concept.   In the example of the game between Andrew and Orville, the less each cares about his own fruit, the less conflict of interest there is.   To illustrate this, Figure 3-1 compares the original game represented in Table 3-1 with a modified version of the same game.   In both games the four possible outcomes are connected with lines for display purposes even though the inability of the players to communicate prevents them from arranging something other than the four elementary outcomes, as they could do in a bargaining game.

TABLE 3-2
Modified Game With Increased
Ease of Generosity

| | | Orville | |
		Keep Orange	Give Orange to Andrew
	Keep Apple	3,3	8,2
Andrew	Give Apple to Orville	2½,6	7½,5

TABLE 3-3
Another Modification
Unequal Ease of Generosity

		Orville	
		Keep Orange	Give Orange to Andrew
	Keep Apple	3,3	8,2
Andrew	Give Apple to Orville	1,6	6,5

The modified game has been constructed by changing the utility schedules of the players so that the utility sacrificed by giving away one's own fruit is halved. Table 3-2 shows the payoff matrix of the modified game. In Pruit's terminology (1965) the ease of generosity is twice as great for both players in the modified game. Since it is easier for the players to be generous to each other, the conflict of interest is less in the modified game.

The comparison of the conflict of interest of two Prisoner's Dilemmas is not as simple if the ease of generosity for one player is greater in one game and greater for the other player in the other game. Table 3-3 displays a new modification of the game between Andrew and Orville, and Figure 3-2 shows both the original and this new game. In the original game (Table 3-1), if Andrew gave away his apple he would sacrifice one unit of his utility (no matter what Orville

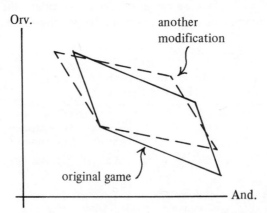

FIGURE 3-2. Two Prisoner's Dilemmas—
Difficult Comparison

did) and provide Orville with 3 extra units of Orville's utility. In the new game (Table 3-3) it costs Andrew twice as much to provide the same gain to Orville. Therefore, it is easier for Andrew to be generous in the original game. For Orville the situation is reversed. Giving away the orange costs him twice as much in the original game although it provides the same bonus to Andrew in both games. Therefore it is easier for Orville to be generous in the new game. So the concept of ease of generosity is not sufficient by itself to determine which of these games has the greater conflict of interest.

This difficulty in measuring conflict of interest in two Prisoner's Dilemma games is closely analogous to the problem of comparing the conflict of interest in two bargaining games with just the concept of the cost of meeting a demand. For some demands the cost in one bargaining game may be higher and for other demands the cost in the other bargaining game may be higher. Rather than begin anew to try to derive a definition with a list of properties that should be satisfied by any procedure to measure conflict of interest in the Prisoner's Dilemma, we can readily generalize the result of the axiomatic process in the bargaining game to cover the Prisoner's Dilemma.

The solution of the axiomatic approach to the bargaining game was to normalize the game based on the best and worst each player could do, and then calculate the area within the unit square which lies beyond the region of feasible agreements. To apply a similar solution to the Prisoner's Dilemma requires only that the appropriate normalization be found, and the appropriate area to measure be determined.

To normalize a Prisoner's Dilemma, the zero and unit points of each player's utility schedule must be determined. As in a bargaining game, the zero point should be what each player can unilaterally guarantee for himself. Thus the outcome which should be placed at the origin is the one in which Andrew keeps his apple and Orville keeps his orange. The unit of the utility schedule in a bargaining game was taken to be the best a player could do in light of the fact that the other player was sure to veto any agreement that did not give him at least his no agreement value. But there is no veto in a Prisoner's Dilemma. It is quite possible, for example, that Andrew would give away his apple without knowing that Orville was keeping his orange. Hence a player can hope to get both pieces of fruit. Therefore in normalizing a Prisoner's Dilemma, the unit of the utility schedule should be taken as the value of getting both pieces of fruit, and the zero point is the value of one's own fruit.

To measure the conflict of interest in a normalized game, the appropriate area must be calculated. In the bargaining game this was the area within the unit square beyond the region of feasible agreements. The analogous area for the Prisoner's Dilemma is the area between the lines $x = 1$, $y = 1$ and the quadrangle of the four possible outcomes. The original Prisoner's Dilemma game between Andrew and Orville is shown in normalized form in Figure 3-3 and the appropriate area is shaded. As in the case of the bargaining game, the conflict of interest of a Prisoner's Dilemma can be calculated without actually normalizing the game. The method is just to take the ratio of the outlying area to the area of the rectangle that becomes the unit square if the game were to be normalized.

This outlying area can be calculated by breaking it into two triangles, as in Figure 3-4. In the original example, the areas of these triangles are $A_1 = \frac{1}{2}(8 - 2)(6 - 4) = 6$ and $A_2 = \frac{1}{2}(6 - 1)$ $(8 - 7) = 2\frac{1}{2}$. The outlying area is therefore $A_1 + A_2 = 6 + 2\frac{1}{2} = 8\frac{1}{2}$. The area of the rectangle which becomes the unit square in the normalized version of the game is $(8 - 3)(6 - 3) = 15$. Thus the conflict of interest of the original Prisoner's Dilemma between Andrew and Orville is the ratio of the outlying area to the area of the rectangle: $8\frac{1}{2}/15 = .57$.

One way to see that the definition of conflict of interest in the Prisoner's Dilemma is intuitively justifiable is to note that the closer the players can come to getting their maximum payoffs by an exchange, the smaller the outlying area is and hence the less conflict of interest

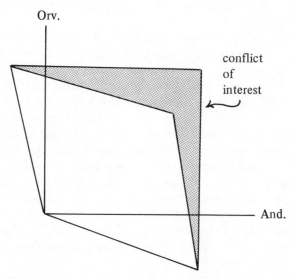

FIGURE 3-3. Normalized Prisoner's Dilemma

Orv.

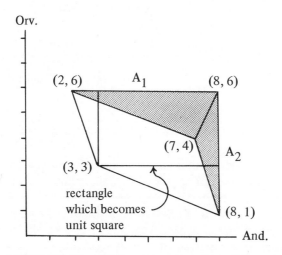

FIGURE 3-4.   Calculating Conflict of Interest
in a Prisoner's Dilemma

there is.   Later this illustration will be expanded to show that the definition takes into account the effects of changing the payoffs of not only the exchange, but of the other three possible outcomes as well.

B. Experimental Tests

GENERAL HYPOTHESIS AND DATA

The procedure to measure conflict of interest in a Prisoner's Dilemma is not testable since it is only a definition.   However, any hypothesis that relates the conflict of interest in a situation to actual behavior is testable.   The main theme—that, other things being equal, the more conflict of interest, the greater the probability of conflictful behavior—can be readily applied to give a general hypothesis.   The general hypothesis for Prisoner's Dilemma games is quite simple: if two Prisoner's Dilemma games are played under similar conditions and differ only in their payoff matrices, then it is more likely that players will make a noncooperative choice in the game with the greater conflict of interest.

The test of the general hypothesis requires a variety of games to be played under the same conditions so that factors other than the entries in the payoff matrix will be held constant.   Although there are now literally dozens of published experimental studies of the Prisoner's Dilemma, nearly all examine the effects of contextual factors

TABLE 3-4
The Symmetric Prisoner's Dilemma

		Player B	
		Defect	Cooperate
	Defect	P,P	T,S
Player A			
	Cooperate	S,T	R,R

such as age, sex, and wording of the instructions.   The only published data suitable for a test of the general hypothesis for Prisoner's Dilemma games appears to be the work of Rapoport and Chammah (1965).   In their first chapter, entitled "In Search of an Index," they pose essentially the same question that is being asked here: how can observed behavior be related to an index derived from the payoff matrix?   Before looking at their suggestions, let us see how well conflict of interest accounts for their experimental data.

Each of the Prisoner's Dilemmas used in Rapoport and Chammah's experiments treats the players symmetrically.   The symmetric payoff matrix is represented with symbolic entries in Table 3-4 with the notation used by Rapoport and Chammah.   Giving away one's fruit is an example of cooperating, and keeping it is an example of defecting.   A specific example of a symmetric Prisoner's Dilemma is shown in Table 3-5.   As usual, the payoff to the row chooser is listed first in each cell.   If a player is the only one to defect he gets T, the temptation to defect, while the other player gets S, the sucker's payoff.   In the example these values are 10 and -10 respectively.   If both defect they each get the punishment P, here equal to -1.   However, if both cooperate both get the reward R, here equal to 5.   In the symmetric case, the definition of the Prisoner's Dilemma is equivalent to the requirements that $T > R > P > S$ and $2R > S + T$.

Note that the cost of cooperating may depend on whether or not the other player cooperates.   In the example in Table 3-5, if the other player cooperates, cooperation costs $T - R = 10 - 5 = 5$ but if he

TABLE 3-5
An Example of a Symmetric Prisoner's Dilemma

		Player B	
		Defect	Cooperate
	Defect	$-1,-1$	$10,-10$
Player A			
	Cooperate	$-10,-10$	5,5

TABLE 3-6
Prisoner's Dilemmas: Experimental Results
(Rapoport and Chammah, 1965, 37 and 47)
Compared to Conflict of Interest

Game	R	S	T	P	% Defect		Conflict of Interest	
					Value	Rank	Value	Rank
II	1	−10	10	−9	23	I	.50	III
I	9	−10	10	−1	27	II	.17	I
IV	1	−2	2	−1	34	III	.44	II
XI	5	−10	10	−1	37	IV	.83	V
XII	1	−10	10	−5	41	V	.80	IV
III	1	−10	10	−1	54	VI	1.49	VI
V	1	−50	50	−1	73	VII	1.88	VII

defects, cooperation costs $P - S = -1 - (-10) = 9$. Of course, the dilemma is that no matter what the other player does it always costs something to cooperate, and yet if neither cooperates both do worse than if both cooperate.

What do people do when confronted with this dilemma? The work of Rapoport and Chammah (1965) provides the answer. In the relevant experiment (call the Pure Matrix Condition) pairs of subjects were given a payoff matrix which they played three hundred times without being allowed to speak to each other. Ten pairs of college students were used for each of seven different Prisoner's Dilemma games. Table 3-6 lists these games in order of frequency of defection. The general hypothesis for Prisoner's Dilemma games predicts that the greater the conflict of interest is, the greater the likelihood the players will defect. The accuracy of this prediction can be assessed by the size of the rank order correlation[1] between the amount of conflict of interest and the percentage of defecting responses. The actual value of the correlation is .86 which signifies a good fit between the hypothesis and the data. There is less than one chance in a hundred this value would be attained by chance. Even though the correlation is high, it is still noticeably less than one. This indicates that the proposed definition of conflict of interest in Prisoner's Dilemma games does not always order games in exactly the same way the experimental results order them. Nevertheless, the data strongly support the conclusion that in a Prisoner's Dilemma the more conflict of interest there is, the less likely are the players to choose a cooperative response.

---

[1] All rank order correlations in this study use Spearman's ρ.

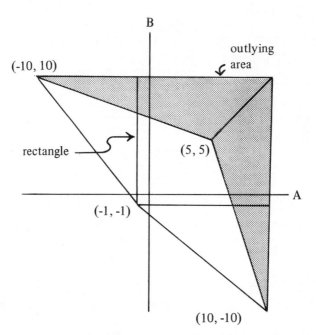

FIGURE 3-5.   A Symmetric
Prisoner's Dilemma

ALTERING CONFLICT OF INTEREST

The conflict of interest of a Prisoner's Dilemma can be altered
by changing any of the four parameters. The effect of changing a
particular parameter can be determined by deriving the formula for
conflict of interest in terms of the parameters. For a symmetric Prisoner's Dilemma, the outlying area can be divided into two equal triangles each with base $T - S$ and height $T - R$, so the total outlying
area is $(T - S)(T - R)$. (See Figure 3-5.) The rectangle that becomes the unit square is already a square and has sides of $T - P$,
with an area of $(T - P)^2$. The conflict of interest of a Prisoner's
Dilemma is the ratio of the outlying area to the area of the rectangle,
and therefore

$$\text{conflict of interest} = \frac{(T - R)(T - S)}{(T - P)^2}.$$

By using this formula it can be shown[2] that conflict of interest (and

---

[2] For R, S, and P the effects can be seen from inspection of the formula.
For T it is necessary to take the partial derivative of conflict of interest, and to
employ the inequalities which define the Prisoner's Dilemma. These inequalities
are $T > R > P > S$, and $2R > S + T$.

hence the predicted percentage of defection) *increases* if:

1. Reward for cooperation R is decreased, or
2. Sucker's payoff S is decreased, or
3. Temptation to defect T is increased, or
4. Punishment for failure to cooperate P is increased.

These predictions are based on the structure of the interaction, rather than the personalities of the players. The identical predictions are made by Rapoport and Chammah (1965, 35–38) and are verified by the data. In light of the fact that the procedure to measure conflict of interest for Prisoner's Dilemma games is simply an extension of the procedure developed for a different type of game, its ability to correctly predict the effects of changing each of the parameters is an indication that a useful definition of conflict of interest is being employed.

An advantage of this definition of conflict of interest is that it combines the effects of all four parameters into a single formula, and thus gives a simple ordering of all Prisoner's Dilemma games. The four predictions above are not sufficient to do this,[3] so Rapoport and Chammah (1965, 43) tried two additional hypotheses, namely that an increase in $(R - S)/(T - S)$ would (a) increase the likelihood of defection, or (b) decrease the likelihood of defection. Actually, if the general hypothesis for conflict of interest in Prisoner's Dilemma games is correct then *both* these *ad hoc* hypotheses are wrong. This is so because it can be shown[4] that the former hypothesis will be wrong if $T + P \geq 2R$ and the latter will be wrong if $T + P \leq 2R$.[5]

Both of the *ad hoc* hypotheses of Rapoport and Chammah are excellent predictors of the percent of defection in the two-person Prisoner's Dilemma. The correlation coefficient are .89 and .93 respectively, and these are higher than the .86 correlation coefficient for conflict of interest. Thus, for this set of data two *ad hoc* hypotheses do better than a specific application of a general theory.

The limitations of the concept of ease of generosity are bypassed by the definition of conflict of interest in the Prisoner's Dilemma. The definition combines the effects of punishment, reward, sucker's payoff, and temptation into a single formula and therefore allows the compari-

---

[3] Other partial indices have been proposed. $T - S$ has been suggested by Rapoport and Orwant (1962). Lave (1965) suggests $S - R$, $T - R$, and $P - R$.

[4] The method is to take the partial derivative of conflict of interest with respect to this ratio, while holding constant Rapoport and Chammah's other ratio $(R - P)/(T - S)$.

[5] More recently, Rapoport (1967a) has proposed a whole family of indices, but since this family contains two unknown coefficients it cannot be tested with the available data.

son of any two Prisoner's Dilemma games. Furthermore, it correctly predicts the effect of changing any one of these parameters. The definition itself was derived by generalizing the unique procedure which satisfied the five axioms for bargaining games, and is quite successful in predicting the rank order of likelihood of defection when Prisoner's Dilemmas are played.

DYNAMICS

Conflict of interest has so far been used to predict the probability that a player will cooperate or defect, regardless of the history of the interaction. But the past, especially the recent past, makes a difference in how a player will act. In particular, the probability that a player will choose to defect on a given play depends in part on what happened on the previous play. For a given game that has been played many times by pairs of players, eight numbers can be computed. These are the probabilities that Player A will defect after a move on which the following happened:

1. Player B cooperated
2. Player A cooperated
3. Player A defected
4. Player B defected
5. Both cooperated
6. Player A cooperated and Player B defected
7. Player A defected and Player B cooperated
8. Both defected.

The fifth number, for example, is the probability that a player will defect after a play on which both players cooperated. Rapoport (1964) uses the suggestive title "perfidy" for this number. The sixth number, the probability that a player will defect after being taken for a sucker, is called "vengefulness." The seventh is the likelihood that a player will defect after receiving the temptation for defecting while the other player cooperated, and can be thought of as representing "greed." The last probability, that of defection after both defected, is called "distrust." (The likelihood that a player will cooperate rather than defect under these last four conditions are appropriately named trustworthiness, forgiveness, repentance, and trust, respectively.) Each of the eight numbers is a probability that a player will defect after a given thing happened on the previous move. This suggests the following eight hypotheses: the more conflict of interest in a game, the larger each of these eight numbers will be. This predicts that the effect of the recent past depends in part on how much conflict of interest there is in the situation. The accuracy of these eight predictions can be assessed by the size of the rank order correlation between the amount of conflict of interest and the probability of defection after each type of move. The experimental data is provided by Rapoport and Chammah (1965, 69 and 77), and the actual value of each of these eight correlation coefficients is at least .61. For each hypothesis there is less than one chance in twenty-five that this value would be attained by chance. Therefore, all of the predictions are confirmed. The effect of the recent past does indeed depend in part on the conflict of interest in a situation. The more conflict of interest there is in a game, the more likely a player is to defect after each of the eight types of history of the previous move.

The second four findings in the Prisoner's Dilemma can be summarized quite simply using the terminology already introduced. When there is high conflict of interest, a player is more likely to display perfidy, vengefulness, greed, and distrust, and less likely to act in a manner of trustworthiness, forgiveness, repentance, and trust. Naturally, in low conflict of interest situations the opposite behavior patterns occur.

These results can be applied to the study of learning. The probabilities that a given choice will follow a certain event (e.g., defection after the other player cooperated) form the elements in a variety of mathematical models of learning. By helping to specify how these numbers differ from one game to another, conflict of interest increases the generality of these models.

The eight results already obtained can also be reworded as statements on how the players learn during the course of their interaction. For example, the first result (which is that a player is more likely to defect after the other player cooperated if there is high conflict of interest) is equivalent to saying that the greater the conflict of interest, the harder it is for one player to learn to respond cooperatively to the other player's cooperation.

THREE-PERSON EQUIVALENT OF THE PRISONER'S DILEMMA

The Prisoner's Dilemma is a two-person game, but the same dilemma of collective action can be generalized to games with more than two players. The definition of conflict of interest can also be generalized. Fortunately, experimental results for the three-person equivalent of the Prisoner's Dilemma are available, so the general hypothesis can be tested in the context of this kind of game.

In the three-person equivalent of the Prisoner's Dilemma the player still has two choices, cooperation or defection, and defection gives a higher payoff than cooperation no matter what the other players do. If only one player defects, he gets T and the other two get S. If two players defect, they receive t and the third gets s. However, if all three defect each gets P, which is lower than the reward R each would get if all three cooperate.

Rapoport (1960) postulates two criteria to explain the percentage of defections in the three-person Prisoner's Dilemma:

1. Advantage of defection over cooperation in expected payoff, and

2. Average advantage over non-defecting players.

In another article Rapoport, Chammah, Dwyer, and Gyr (1962) advance three more criteria:

3. Comparison of expected gain to self and to the maker of the opposite choice,

4. Comparison of expected gain to self and others in the same outcome, and

5. Frequency of defection determined by minimax strategy.

Having calculated the indices based upon these criteria, the authors find that the fourth criterion gives the best fit. Algebraically this index is $-i = 2(T - S) + 2(t - s)$.

The definition of conflict of interest proposed here for the normalized three-person equivalent of the Prisoner's Dilemma is simply the volume between $x = 1$, $y = 1$, $z = 1$ and the region defined by the eight points of the game.[6] The normalization, as before, is $P = 0$ and $T = 1$. Algebraically this is

$$\text{conflict of interest} = \frac{(T - s)^3 - (t - s)(R - s)(T - S)}{(T - P)^3}$$

for the three-person equivalent of the Prisoner's Dilemma.

Rapoport et al. (1962, Table 6, p. 46) report the results of experiments in which each of six three-person groups played eight games in random order for 800 turns without communication. Table 3-7

---

[6] Conflict of interest in the n-person bargaining game is also easy to generalize from the two-person case. It is simply the proportion of the joint demand hypervolume which is infeasible. This is not very difficult to calculate if the utilities for all the feasible agreements are known.

TABLE 3-7

Three-Person Equivalent of Prisoner's Dilemmas:
Experimental Results (Rapoport *et al.*, 1962, 46)
Compared to Conflict of Interest and −i

Game	R	S	T	s	t	P	% Defect		Conflict of Interest		−i	
							Value	Rank	Value	Rank	Value	Rank
9	1	−2	2	−2	2	−1	75.4	I	.59	I	16	I
12	1	−2	4	−2	4	−1	86.3	II	.86	II	24	II– III
16	1	−4	4	−4	4	−1	86.7	III	1.53	VI	32	IV– VI
13	1	−2	6	−2	6	−1	88.0	IV	.93	III	32	IV– VI
11	1	−6	6	−6	6	−1	88.1	V– VI	2.10	VII	48	VII– VIII
14	1	−6	6	−6	6	−3	88.1	V– VI	.99	IV	48	VII– VIII
10	1	−4	2	−4	2	−1	88.2	VII	1.33	V	24	II– III
15	1	−6	2	−6	2	−1	90.1	VIII	2.37	VIII	32	IV– VI

lists these games in order of defection, and shows the value and rank of each game on the magnitude of conflict of interest and the index −i. The rank order correlation of −i and the percentage of defection is .49. The rank order correlation of the proposed definition of conflict of interest and the percentage of defection is .78. The probability these would be attained by chance is more than one in ten for the former value and one in eighty for the latter. Thus the proposed definition of conflict of interest is a better predictor of the subjects' behavior.

A comparison of the two indices reveals that −i is independent of R and P, but conflict of interest is a function of all six parameters. The partial ability of −i to predict the percentage of defection is probably due to the fact that R did not change at all and P had the same value in seven of the eight games used. If for a given game the reward for cooperation R were lowered, or the punishment for defection P were raised, common sense and the experience of the two-person Prisoner's Dilemma games suggest the players would be more likely to defect. The same prediction is supported by conflict of interest (which would increase), but not by the index −i (which would remain unchanged). Therefore in the three-person equivalent of the Prisoner's

Dilemma game the proposed definition of conflict of interest is better than the index —i in two respects: it is a better predictor of behavior in eight experimental games, and it incorporates the effects of two parameters which were held nearly constant in these eight games.   Furthermore, the definition of conflict of interest in Prisoner's Dilemma games has the virtue of being a generalization of a definition derived from a list of intuitively justifiable properties about conflict of interest in a different type of strategic interaction, namely bargaining games.

C. Summary

The Prisoner's Dilemma is a game played without communication or the possibility of making binding commitments, and is characterized by the property that if two individuals pursue their own interests, both do worse than they could if they were generous to each other.   Conflict of interest can be defined for a Prisoner's Dilemma by generalizing the procedure for bargaining games which was developed by an axiomatic approach.   The appropriate normalization sets the zero point of a player's utility at what he can unilaterally guarantee himself, and sets the unit point at the tempting payoff for defecting while the other player cooperates.   With this normalization, the conflict of interest in a Prisoner's Dilemma is the area between the quadrangle defined by the four possible outcomes, and the lines $x = 1$ and $y = 1$.

The following results have been verified for the Prisoner's Dilemma with data from laboratory experiments conducted by Rapoport and his colleagues:

1. The more conflict of interest, the more likely it is that a player will defect (the general hypothesis).

2. The likelihood of defection increases with a decrease in the reward for cooperation or the sucker's payoff, and with an increase in the temptation to defect or the punishment for failure to cooperate, all as predicted by the general hypothesis applied to the formula for conflict of interest.

3. The effect of the previous move depends on the conflict of interest.   For example, the more conflict of interest, the more "perfidy," "vengefulness," "greed," and "distrust."   A corollary of this is that learning to cooperate is harder in a high conflict of interest situation.

4. In the three-person equivalent of the Prisoner's Dilemma, the more conflict of interest the greater the likelihood of defection.   The proposed definition of conflict of interest is a better predictor of actual

behavior than any previously proposed index for the three-person equivalent of the Prisoner's Dilemma.

5. Also in the three-person equivalent of the Prisoner's Dilemma, conflict of interest incorporates all six parameters of the game whereas the best published alternative index is insensitive to changes in two of them.

It is rare in the social sciences for an intuitively justifiable concept to be derived from formal considerations and still be useful for predicting empirical results.   This, however, is the case for conflict of interest.

The next problem to be considered is how to apply the concept to the study of political arenas which are much more complex than laboratory experiments.   Chapter 4 deals with the nature of this problem, and the actual political applications are discussed in Part II.

4

Conflict of Interest
in the Study of Politics

This chapter deals with the use of the concept of conflict of interest as an empirical tool in the study of politics. The first section discusses how to apply the concept to a given political arena. It deals with the requirements for an ideal test of a prediction using this concept and with tactics for relaxing these requirements. The second section treats the different types of conflict of interest which reflect different aspects of a strategic interaction. These topics provide the necessary preparation for the treatment of political applications. These applications are discussed in Part II.

A. Applying the Concept

REQUIREMENTS FOR AN IDEAL TEST OF A PREDICTION

The requirements for an ideal test of a prediction of political behavior using the concept of conflict of interest can be conveniently listed under the seven headings in Table 4-1. When each of these requirements is fulfilled, the researcher is able to test the ability of conflict of interest to help predict political behavior. In this section these conditions are examined one by one to determine how readily they can be met. In the next section, some techniques that relax the most difficult conditions are discussed.

1. *Model of the Strategic Interaction.* If conflict of interest is to be used to test a prediction in a given situation, the type of strategic interaction in that situation must be specified. Suppose the concept of conflict of interest is going to be used to predict how a Congressman will vote on a bill. The model of the strategic interaction between members of Congress must specify the participants (e.g., Representatives, or members of both Houses of Congress, or Congress and the President); the range of strategies they possess (e.g., to vote or also to introduce an amendment); the outcome that results when everyone has selected his strategy (e.g., whether a particular vote requires a simple majority or two-thirds); and the utility of the various outcomes (e.g., whether a Congressman prefers to win with an overwhelming majority or whether a bare majority is just as good).

The model must allow for varying degrees of conflict of interest among the participants. Otherwise it would be impossible to determine the effects of conflict of interest on their behavior. Unfortunately many of the game theory models that have been devised to study political processes assume a fixed level of conflict of interest, even though they do not all assume the process is a zero-sum game.

The institutional setting of a political process often helps make model building easier. For example, a model of the coalition formation process in the Senate can use the simple assumption that "each Senator shall have one Vote," as stated in Article I of the Constitution of the United States. Compare the well-defined institutional setting of the American Senate with the procedure in the British Cabinet. According to Sampson (1965, 128), "There are no rules about how to run a cabinet. . . . Discussions hardly ever come to a vote: if there is disagreement, they return to the subject, giving and taking until either

TABLE 4-1

A list of requirements for an ideal test of a prediction using conflict of interest:

1. Model of the strategic interaction
2. Definition of conflict of interest
3. Hypotheses relating conflict of interest to behavior
4. Determination of the possible outcomes
5. Measurement of the participants' utilities for these outcomes
6. Observation of behavior under different amounts of conflict of interest
7. Statistical control of other influences on behavior

a majority view takes shape, or—in extremity—a minister resigns." Of course, unlike in the Senate, such a majority view is not likely to count each minister equally, so a model for the British Cabinet would not be as easy to construct as one for the American Senate.

2. *Definition of Conflict of Interest.* If the strategic interaction is not a bargaining game or a Prisoner's Dilemma, conflict of interest remains to be formally defined. The definition is far from being arbitrary, however, provided it is a natural generalization of the way conflict of interest has already been defined for these two types of games. In particular, the amount of conflict of interest in any situation of strategic interaction should be the ratio of two areas in the utility space. The first area is the one beyond the region of possible outcomes, and the second is the area of the rectangle which becomes the unit square after normalization. The normalization must always be based upon the most reasonable values for the zero and unit points of a player's utility schedules in that specific situation.

In addition, the new definition of conflict of interest in the new situation of strategic interaction should satisfy as many of the five axioms for bargaining games as are relevant to the new situation. The first three will almost always be relevant, and hence be required. These three are symmetry (invariance with respect to interchange of the labels of the players); independence (independence with respect to choice of representation of the players' utility schedules); and continuity (if two games are almost alike they should have almost the same conflict of interest, and have exactly the same in the limiting case). Of the last two axioms used to derive the definition of conflict of interest in bargaining games, one was introduced as a convenience (boundedness), and the other applies in its present form specifically to bargaining games (additivity). Incidentally, the definition of conflict of interest in the Prisoner's Dilemma satisfies symmetry, independence, and continuity, as it should.[1] As it turns out, there is no upper bound to the amount of conflict of interest a Prisoner's Dilemma can have.

Yet another requirement exists for the definition of conflict of interest in a new type of strategic interaction and might be called consistency. If a particular game G is either a bargaining game or a Prisoner's Dilemma and is at the same time an example of the new type of interaction, then there are two ways to measure the amount of conflict of interest of G. One is to use the old definition for the bargaining game or the Prisoner's Dilemma (whichever G is), and

---

[1] Harris (1969) provides a way of classifying 2×2 games that might be useful in generalizing conflict of interest beyond the Prisoner's Dilemma.

the other is to apply the definition of conflict of interest for the new kind of situation, treating G as just an example of that kind of interaction. The axiom of *consistency* says that the new definition must give the same answer as the old one for G, because both definitions are equally applicable.

Therefore even though the conflict of interest must be defined anew for each new type of strategic interaction, the definition is very far from being arbitrary. It must satisfy three sets of conditions:

a. It must be the ratio of two areas in the utility space, each of which must have certain given properties.

b. It must satisfy the old axioms of symmetry, independence, and continuity.

c. It must satisfy the new axiom of consistency which requires that whenever a game can be regarded as an example of two kinds of strategic interactions, the two relevant definitions of conflict of interest must give the same answer.

As an example, consider a two-person game just like the bargaining game except that randomizations between elementary agreements are not allowed. Then the obvious way to normalize the game is still with the best and worst each player can do. The obvious way to generalize the infeasible demand area is to take every point for which there is no feasible agreement that both prefer to that point. One

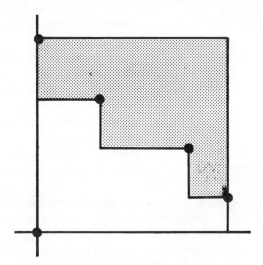

FIGURE 4-1. Game Without
Randomizations

such game is illustrated in Figure 4-1. Conflict of interest for this type of game can be defined as before as the proportion of the unit square that is in the infeasible demand area. This definition satisfies each of the conditions set forth above, including consistency which applies when the game happens to have a convex boundary. Disallowing randomization can never decrease the conflict of interest of a bargaining game. In the extreme case this kind of game can have a conflict of interest of one, which helps to explain why the maximum conflict of interest of a bargaining game was taken to be one-half.

3. *Hypotheses Relating Conflict of Interest to Behavior.* In order to use conflict of interest to predict behavior, it is obvious that specific hypotheses are necessary. The basic theme is simply that other things being equal, the more conflict of interest there is, the more probable it is that conflictful behavior will result. The specific meaning of conflictful behavior will differ from one political process to another, of course, but usually there are types of behavior which are clearly conflictful and hence some hypotheses are easy to specify.

4. *Determination of Possible Outcomes.* An essential part of a model of a political process is the listing of the possible outcomes. Determining these outcomes may be a difficult empirical problem. In an abstract game such as the Prisoner's Dilemma it will be easy because there are only a very limited number of things that can happen. However, in an actual political arena, there may be a vast number of possible outcomes (such as different legislation in Congress on a given issue) and an important part of the political process may be the search for still more feasible outcomes. A technique for dealing with this problem is discussed later.

5. *Measurement of the Participants' Utilities for These Outcomes.* Here is the most difficult empirical problem of all. Since conflict of interest depends directly on the way the preferences of the participants are related, the participants' utility schedules are crucial. Some tactics for dealing with the problems of measuring utility are considered later.

6. *Observation of Behavior under Different Amounts of Conflict of Interest.* It is insufficient to observe behavior under conditions of constant conflict of interest, because, to test a hypothesis, behavior under conditions of high conflict of interest must be compared to behavior under conditions of low conflict of interest. Observation of political behavior is sometimes exceedingly difficult because the participants may have a strong incentive to hide what goes on in a smoke-filled room, but often the observation is as simple as noting how a Congressman voted on a roll call. Some types of behavior such as public expressions of sentiment are easy to observe but difficult to code in

terms of specific strategy choices.   However, many other forms of political behavior are almost as simple to code as a roll call vote.

7. *Statistical Control of Other Influences on Behavior.*   When
testing predictions by comparing situations of high and low conflict
of interest it is necessary to assume that "other things are equal."   The
problem this causes is illustrated by the finding of Sampson and Kardush
(1965) that young Negroes playing a Prisoner's Dilemma defect less
often than whites playing the same game.   Therefore it is conceivable
that young Negroes would defect less often even when they played
a game with slightly more conflict of interest.   This would result in
less defection being observed in the game with the greater conflict
of interest.   Such an observation would not represent a failure of the
general hypothesis for Prisoner's Dilemmas, but rather a failure of the
ceteris paribus assumption which a test of that hypothesis requires.

The question is how to control influences on behavior (such as
race and saliency) that lead to differences in behavior and are independent of the effects of conflict of interest.   Several methods are available.   The most direct one is rigid control of the outside influence.
For example, both groups of subjects could be given both games to
play, and the general hypothesis would predict that Negroes would
defect less than other Negroes, and whites would defect less than other
whites, in the game with less conflict of interest.   A second method
of controlling extraneous influences on behavior is randomization.   In
the laboratory example, the subjects assigned to the two games can
be chosen at random so the Negroes and whites play the high conflict
of interest game in roughly the same proportion as the low conflict
of interest game.   In Congress, one might assume that the proportion
of Negro Congressmen does not change significantly from one session
to the next and therefore no problem would arise on this account.   Of
course the Negro Congressmen may vote quite differently on some
issues from most other Congressmen because they have different goals,
but conflict of interest already incorporates the effect of the goals of
the players.

The *ceteris paribus* assumption requires that factors not reflected
in conflict of interest remain unchanged.   This still allows considerable
freedom because a variety of strategic factors are reflected in the single
variable of conflict of interest.   These factors include the strategies
available to the participants, the outcomes that occur when strategies
are selected, and the preferences for each outcome.   Therefore, many
types of changes in the situation are allowed, including the threats
available to the participants, the costs of using these threats, addition
or elimination of some possible outcomes, and how much the partici-

pants care about the various issues at stake. Changes of this type are reflected in the amount of conflict of interest, and hence their effects can be tested with this concept if the factors not reflected in the conflict of interest are controlled.

TECHNIQUES TO RELAX THE REQUIREMENTS

Since the two most difficult requirements for testing predictions of political behavior using conflict of interest are the determination of possible outcomes and the measurement of the participants' utilities for these outcomes, techniques for relaxing these two requirements will be considered.

In order to examine what the investigator can do if only limited information on the possible outcomes is available, use will be made of the example of a bilateral treaty between the United States and the U.S.S.R. The fact that each of these two actors is a group rather than an individual adds no special problem provided that each acts consistently and therefore can be regarded as having a utility schedule. The negotiation process can be regarded as a two-actor bargaining game, and it can be assumed for simplicity that it does not matter to the players how a particular agreement is reached.

Even though the investigator is not able to determine each of the possible agreements, he is likely to be able to identify at least four outcomes, namely:

a. No agreement,
b. The Russian draft treaty,
c. The American draft treaty, and
d. Some compromise treaty on the upper right boundary of the region of feasible outcomes (i.e. one which cannot be rewritten without making it less satisfactory to at least one of the players).

It shall be assumed for the sake of discussion that both sides rank these outcomes in the order of their own draft being most preferred, the compromise next, then the other's draft, and least of all no agreement. For the normalized version of the game, the payoffs are $A = (0,0)$, $B = (1,y_1)$, $C = (x_1,1)$, and $D = (x_2,y_2)$. Now suppose the investigator is able to go to both actors and get an answer to the following question: "How sure do you have to be of getting your draft approved before you would be unwilling to settle for compromise D?" This is precisely the question that defines the utility of D relative to 0 and 1, so the answer will be x_2 for the first player and y_2 for the second player. This determines a single point on the boundary of the region although the shape of the region is still undetermined.

This one point is enough to set an upper bound and a lower bound on the amount of conflict of interest in the bargaining game. If the Russians would have to be at least 60% sure of getting their draft before they would prefer not to settle for the compromise and the Americans would have to be 70% sure of getting *their* draft before not settling for that compromise, then $D = (.6, .7)$. Since the region of feasible outcomes is assumed to be convex, no matter what other compromises are possible, the maximum conflict of interest is .35 (when each side is actually indifferent between the other's draft treaty and no agreement, making $x_1 = 0$ and $y_1 = 0$ as in Figure 4-2), and the minimum conflict of interest is .24 (when $x_1 = .2$ and $y_1 = .4$, as in Figure 4-3). Thus the investigator knows that the conflict of interest is between about $\frac{1}{4}$ and $\frac{1}{3}$. The point of this exercise is that even if only a very few of the many possible outcomes in a bargaining game can be determined the conflict of interest can be measured within reasonable bounds. This is an important feature of the definition of conflict of interest because it means that hypotheses that employ it can be tested with only limited information about the actual situation.

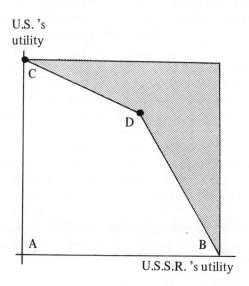

U.S. 's
utility

C

D

A   B

U.S.S.R. 's utility

FIGURE 4-2. Maximum Conflict
of Interest

U.S. 's
utility

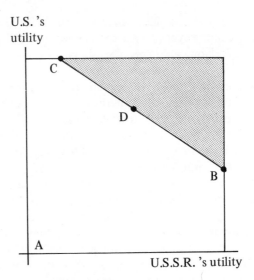

U.S.S.R. 's utility

FIGURE 4-3.   Minimum Conflict
of Interest

The most difficult problem in employing the concept of conflict of interest is the measurement of the participants' utility schedules. Four procedures are available: observing choices in a lottery, interviewing, using objective criteria, and analyzing patterns of past behavior.

a. The ideal method is to *observe a person's choice when confronted with a simple lottery,* since this is how utility has been defined in Chapter 1.   However, when a Congressman, for example, has to choose between a 60% chance of getting bill A (or no bill) and being sure of getting bill B, the probabilities are subjective.

b. It is difficult for the researcher to determine how a Congressman perceives the subjective probabilities except by the second procedure, which is *interviewing.*   Once interviewing is undertaken the problem can be simplified because the Congressman can be asked what he would do if the choices were such and such.   (A substitute for interviewing an actor may be to interview someone who is in a position to make an expert judgment on the preferences of the actor, such as the chief of the actor's staff.)   A form of this method is examined in the appendix to Chapter 5.

c. Nevertheless, the problems of reliably determining preferences in an interview are sufficiently great to suggest consideration of the third procedure: *the use of objective criteria to impute an individual's preferences.* This is the method used in laboratory games when it is assumed that the pennies given the subject are the only relevant determinant of his utility. While this assumption is open to considerable doubt, it may well be meaningful to use objective criteria to impute the preferences of a political actor. A Congressman from a rural district that has a serious water shortage may occasionally vote against proposals to provide more water at lower costs to the consumer, but the researcher can be reasonably sure that this is a question of legislative tactics rather than a preference for less water. The imputation of a strong preference for more and cheaper water is a safe assumption for such a Congressman.

d. The final method of assigning utilities is to *analyze patterns of past political behavior using any one of a variety of statistical techniques* that are available for the analysis of patterns. These techniques can be used to provide a simple description of a Congressman's voting record, for example by revealing that he usually voted with the liberals on social welfare issues and with the isolationists on foreign policy issues. The problem here is that in trying to determine his true preferences it is difficult to say whether, for example, he actually preferred an isolationist policy or whether he consistently traded his foreign policy votes to an isolationist in return for the isolationist's votes on some other issue.

The state of the art of measuring utilities is still rather rudimentary, these four methods notwithstanding. This problem is not unique to the study of conflict of interest; it extends to many other concepts of game theory as well.

One way to ease the difficulty of measuring utilities is to determine only the order of the preferences of each actor, rather than the relative spacing of the preferences. This gives an ordinal utility schedule: it may say that the U.S. finds the compromise treaty to be preferable to the U.S.S.R.'s draft and not as good as its own draft, but it does not specify whether the compromise is almost as desirable as its own draft or whether it is nearly as undesirable as the U.S.S.R.'s draft. The amount of conflict of interest in the situation obviously depends on more than the ordering of the alternatives since the closer the compromise is to each player's first choice the less conflict of interest there is between them. Thus, ordinal utilities are insufficient to determine the amount of conflict of interest in a situation.

Fortunately, it is not always necessary to determine the exact amount of conflict of interest. It may be sufficient to determine whether one situation has more conflict of interest than another, so that the exact amounts in each may not have to be measured. If a hypothesis says that a certain kind of behavior is more likely the more conflict of interest there is, a test of this prediction requires only that it be known which of two observed situations has more conflict of interest.

To determine which has more conflict of interest, ordinal utility schedules are sometimes enough—provided that a utility schedule in one game is comparable to a utility schedule in another. The simplest way of achieving this comparability is to observe the same players in a situation before and after some change is introduced. Thus, if the United States discovers that the failure to reach an agreement on a treaty is a worse outcome than it previously thought, the no agreement point is lowered and the conflict of interest with the U.S.S.R. is decreased. The observer cannot yet say by how much the conflict of interest has been reduced, but he does know that it has been reduced. Therefore, a prediction—such as the more conflict of interest there is, the more hostile the communications on the subject will be—can be tested by comparing the messages before and after the U.S. change.

Incidentally, there is no need to compare the utility schedule of the United States to that of the U.S.S.R. All utility comparisons are made for the preferences between different outcomes for a single actor. While the normalization of a game seems to equate the zero and unit of one player's utility to the zero and unit of another's, this comparison need never occur if the definition of conflict of interest as the ratio of two areas is used. Measurement of conflict of interest does not require an interpersonal comparison of utility.

In comparing two situations with only ordinal utilities an interpersonal comparison can be avoided if the participants are the same. If two situations differ in some specific way it may be easy to say which one has more conflict of interest. Many rules for doing this have already been developed in the chapters on the bargaining game and the Prisoner's Dilemma. An example of these rules in the bargaining game is that an expansion of the region of feasible agreements will lower the conflict of interest provided the maximum either player can hope to achieve is not raised. An example in the Prisoner's Dilemma is that an increase in the temptation to defect will increase the conflict of interest. Once a definition of conflict of interest is made for a new type of strategic interaction it is not difficult to specify additional rules on how the conflict of interest is affected by a variety of ordinal changes in the situation.

These techniques to relax the requirements for testing predictions of political behavior that employ the concept of conflict of interest hardly solve all the problems which arise when an actual political arena is studied. But perhaps they can be of some help.

B. Types of Conflict of Interest

So far the idea of conflict of interest has been treated as a single concept. Actually, in a given situation conflict of interest can be employed to distinguish a number of different aspects of the strategic interaction and thereby refine the analysis. Various types of conflict of interest can be derived from three distinctions: relative vs. absolute, informed vs. uninformed, and total vs. restricted. The central concept, and the one which has been the sole subject of the exposition so far, is based on the first half of the three pairs, making it relative, informed, and total. Whenever the term "conflict of interest" is used without qualification these adjectives are assumed to apply.

RELATIVE VS. ABSOLUTE

The first distinction is the one between relative and absolute conflict of interest. Here is a simple example. Suppose two players are allowed to keep a sum of money if they can agree on how to split it. This is, of course, a bargaining game. If each player is indifferent between getting a sum of money in this range and an even chance of getting twice as much, the region of feasible agreements will have a flat boundary.

The (relative) conflict of interest is ½ because the area beyond the region of feasible agreements is one half of the unit square regardless of the size of the sum to be divided. The structure of the interaction is the same whether the sum is one dollar or two dollars, and therefore the conflict of interest relative to the stakes of the game is the same (see Figures 4-4 and 4-5). On the other hand, the absolute conflict

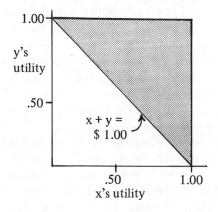

FIGURE 4-4.   One dollar to be split

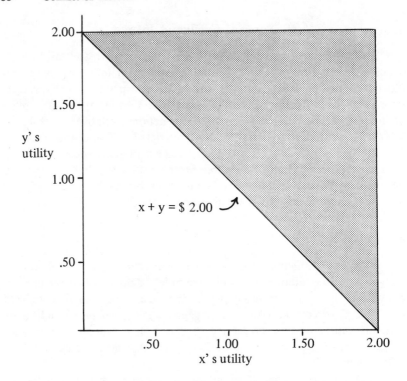

FIGURE 4-5.   Two dollars to be split

of interest is greater when the stakes are higher.   Some of the common sense mistakes of the Practical Man in Chapter 2 were caused by his failure to make this analytic distinction.

The relative conflict of interest compares the divergent to the common interests while the absolute conflict of interest considers only the magnitude of the divergent interests.   When the sum to be split is two dollars, both the common and divergent interests increase, so the relative conflict of interest is unchanged but the absolute conflict of interest (based only on the divergent interests) increases.

There is a simple graphical interpretation for both the relative and absolute forms.   The relative conflict of interest is the familiar ratio of the two areas.   The absolute conflict of interest is just the first area, namely the area beyond the region of feasible agreements. This area quadruples when the stakes of the game are doubled for both players, and hence the absolute conflict of interest is quadrupled. The relative conflict of interest remains unchanged because the area of the rectangle which becomes the unit square also quadruples and hence the ratio of the two areas remains the same.

Relative conflict of interest is measured as a pure number because it is the ratio of two areas.   Absolute conflict of interest is measured in terms of an area of the utility space and hence in terms of player 1's utility times player 2's utility.   In this example utility is proportional to money and hence the units can be taken as dollars times dollars. When one dollar is to be split the absolute conflict of interest is $\frac{1}{2}$ (dollar)^2. When the sum to be split is two dollars, the absolute conflict of interest is 2 (dollars)^2.   These values of absolute conflict of interest can be derived by calculating the shaded areas of Figures 4-4 and 4-5.

If players are given their choice of games they should not necessarily choose the game with the least absolute conflict of interest or the one with the least relative conflict of interest.   For example, two players would probably rather play a regular bargaining game to split up two dollars than play a constrained bargaining game to split up a dime, the latter of which has the requirement that each player gets no more than a nickel.   The dime game has no conflict of interest of either kind because both players can get their maximum, a nickel, at the same time.   The two dollar game has more relative and absolute conflict of interest than the dime game (which has none of either), but the expected gain to each player in the two dollar game is probably much greater.

One interesting property of absolute conflict of interest in a bargaining game is that it does not depend upon the null point as long as the null point is worse for each of the players than the other player's most preferred outcome.   This is one reason absolute conflict of interest might be regarded as a more elementary concept than relative conflict of interest.   However, in this study the relative form has been treated as the fundamental concept because relative conflict of interest takes into account both the common and divergent interests of the players rather than just their divergent interests.   Thus the predictions in this study are based on relative conflict of interest.

INFORMED VS. UNINFORMED

Utilities are by definition subjective.   They depend upon the actors' beliefs about what the various possible outcomes will mean to them.   Therefore the amount of information available to the participants affects the payoffs and this in turn affects the amount of conflict of interest.

Rarely do the actors have complete knowledge or no knowledge at all of the various outcomes.   Therefore, the idea of informed vs. uninformed conflict of interest should not be regarded as a simple dichotomy. Instead, conflict of interest depends on just what the players know about the payoffs. (They never know about the other player's next move.) Given the structure of the game and the beliefs of the players about the payoffs, conflict of interest can be calculated. If the players learn more about the possible outcomes, conflict of interest can change.

Often the question of how much knowledge the players have of the meaning of the various possible outcomes can be avoided by determining from the players themselves how much they value each of the possible outcomes. That is why the term "conflict of interest" when used without qualification can be thought of as informed conflict of interest, i.e. the conflict of interest which exists given the information about payoffs which is available to the players.

TOTAL VS. RESTRICTED

The third distinction is between conflict of interest in the total situation and conflict of interest in a part of the situation. In the House of Representatives, for example, there might be considerable conflict of interest over a civil rights bill, but the conservative southerners may have little conflict of interest among themselves. In this instance, the total conflict of interest in the House is high while the restricted conflict of interest among conservative southerners is low.

Restricted conflict of interest can be regarded as the conflict of interest in the situation of strategic interaction that results from a limitation on the total situation. The limitation may be either on the number of participants (such as the consideration of the interaction among just conservative southerners), or on the strategies available to the participants (such as a rule against introducing amendments), or on both.

For a given set of restrictions, the amount of conflict of interest can be calculated by constructing a new game which includes these restrictions and measuring the (total) conflict of interest in the new game. The restricted conflict of interest can be greater or less than the total conflict of interest depending on the nature of the restrictions. For example, even in an n-person zero-sum game, some of the players may have low restricted conflict of interest among themselves if they can combine to form a winning coalition against the other players.

Restricted conflict of interest is especially relevant in complex situations. In many political processes the participants are faced with a strategic problem so complicated that they are able to deal with it only in a piecemeal fashion. They may focus their attention on only a few of their possible strategies and/or on only a few of the other participants. If so, the appropriate restricted conflict of interest may be useful for predicting their behavior in their self-restricted interaction.

C. Summary

Using the concept of conflict of interest as an empirical tool in the study of politics involves a variety of difficulties. An ideal test of a prediction using this concept must fulfill a variety of requirements, some of which are quite challenging. The two that are likely to be hardest are the determination of the possible outcomes and the measurement of the participants' utilities for these outcomes. Fortunately, these two requirements can be relaxed. Knowing about only a few of the outcomes may be sufficient to attain a good approximation of the amount of conflict of interest in a situation. With regard to measuring utilities, sometimes objective characteristics of an outcome can be used to impute subjective preferences, and in addition the knowledge of ordinal preferences is often sufficient.

Conflict of interest can also be applied to more than one aspect of a strategic interaction to refine the analysis. Various types of conflict of interest can be derived from three distinctions: relative vs. absolute, informed vs. uninformed, and total vs. restricted. Relative conflict of interest remains unchanged when the stakes for both players double, but absolute conflict of interest increases. In other words, relative conflict of interest compares the divergent interests to the common interests of the players while absolute conflict of interest measures only the magnitude of the divergent interests. Informed conflict of interest is based on the utilities of the outcomes as the players perceive them. Finally, total conflict of interest refers to the interaction among all the actors with their complete range of strategy choices, and restricted conflict of interest is what results if the number of actors and/or the range of strategies are restricted. The fundamental concept is relative, informed, and total. The other combinations are useful for special purposes and are formally definable in relation to the fundamental definition of conflict of interest in the interaction.

A final point should be made here about a limitation on the use of conflict of interest. Ideally the amount of conflict of interest in one situation should be directly comparable to the amount in any other situation no matter how different the type of strategic interaction. However, present theory is not this strong. Conflict of interest is comparable in any two games of the same strategic type, but it is not possible to compare two different types of games. It may thus be possible to say whether there is greater conflict of interest over one issue or another in Congress (both voting games) or over one or another treaty issue between the United States and the U.S.S.R. (both bargaining games), but it is not yet possible to say whether a given situation in Congress has more or less conflict of interest than a given treaty issue between the two nations. Of course, this is not too great a handicap because the resultant forms of conflictful behavior are not readily comparable anyway. The useful activity is to predict different kinds of behavior in different arenas with the same concept, and this is what the formalization of conflict of interest will allow.

Part II

POLITICAL
APPLICATIONS

5

Congressional Conference Committee

A. Introduction

The tools developed in Part I of this study of conflict of interest are not sufficient to analyze each and every political process. However, two types of strategic interaction that can readily be treated in terms of conflict of interest are the bargaining game and the Prisoner's Dilemma. One important political process which closely resembles one of these types of interaction (the bargaining game) is the process of adjusting differences between the two chambers of Congress.

The institutional arrangement for this process of adjustment is the Congressional conference committee. The historical development and current functioning of this conference system is the subject of this chapter. First, the evolution of the system over six centuries in England and the United States is recounted. This evolution is especially interesting because it can be analyzed as a slow progression toward fulfilling the assumptions of the two-person bargaining game model, with the greatest progress made in a period of extreme conflict of interest.   Next, the assumptions of the bargaining game model are spelled out as they apply to the Congressional conference committee and the adequacy of these assumptions is assessed.   Finally, a case study of a recent conference dispute is analyzed.   An unusually bitter and complex dispute is chosen in order to evaluate the contributions and limitations of a conflict of interest analysis.   Also provided is an Appendix that treats the empirical problems involved in a statistical test of a theory of conflict of interest as it might be applied to the Congressional conference committee.

B. History of the Congressional Conference Committee

ORIGINS OF THE SYSTEM

The antecedents of the Congressional conference committee date back to the fourteenth century when the English Parliament first assumed its bicameral character.   (The following account is taken from McCown, 1927).   Records of the House of Lords indicate that by 1378 it was already an established practice for two committees, one from each house, to meet together and then for each to report back to its own house.   Thus institutional arrangements for resolving conflicts of interest between the two chambers were developed almost as soon as the need arose.

The procedures employed a step-by-step process aimed at eventual resolution of the differences between the houses.   Messages were sent back and forth between the houses.   If the Commons, for example, wished to send a message to the Lords, it would request a conference. The only business at this meeting would be the reading and transmittal of a report from the Commons giving reasons for its position.   The Lords could then request another such so-called "simple" conference in which its reasons would be presented.   The third conference, if needed, could be requested by the chamber that had requested the original meeting.   This time the conference would be "free," meaning that the delegates were allowed to enter into free discussion in an effort to bring the two houses into agreement.

The use of the conference system in England grew throughout the fifteenth, sixteenth, and seventeenth centuries, but the significance of conferences died out with the development of the cabinet system in the eighteenth century.   The cabinet exercised legislative as well as executive leadership, so it could coordinate the activities of the two chambers and thereby eliminate the need for a conference system. However, it was in the seventeenth century, when the conference system was at its height in England, that the American colonial legislatures developed their systems of operation. Not surprisingly, many of the colonial legislatures employed conference committees to help adjust differences between their two chambers.

DEVELOPMENT OF THE SYSTEM IN AMERICA

At the beginning of the first session of the first Congress, on April 7, 1789, the day after a quorum was first secured, the Senate appointed a committee to prepare rules to govern in case of conference, and soon thereafter the House of Representatives did likewise. The result of this joint committee's report was a joint rule that provided for a free conference in case of differences in a bill as passed by both chambers. Thus the Congress lost no time in setting up the institutional arrangements for dealing with potential conflicts of interest between the House and the Senate.

At first the conference committees were not very powerful, but as they demonstrated their value, they were granted more and more privileges. Since the practices that give the conference system its power were established through custom and were only later formalized in rules or firm precedents, it is impossible to determine exactly when each of these practices originated. However, six elements of the modern Congressional conference committee system were developed by the middle of the nineteenth century. These are:

1. The conference report must be accepted or rejected as a whole, and its acceptance implies agreement with all of its recommendations.

2. The conference proceedings are held in secret.

3. The committee can delay its report until the final hours of the session, thereby preventing detailed consideration of the report or a second conference.

4. When the report is presented it has highest privilege of precedence and can displace all other legislation.

5. Conference committee members by custom are chosen by seniority from the committees in charge of the bill, making the conference system, in effect, an extension of the system of standing legislative committees (Gross, 1953, 320ff.).

6. There are special procedures available to speed a bill to conference.

These practices and understandings can all be found in the records of Congress in the middle of the nineteenth century. To quote McCown (1927, 72–73):

For some years [before about 1853] antagonism between the two Houses had been increasing on certain questions. The conference committee was being used more and more in a desperate effort to bring the Senate and House together on the essentials of government. The leaders learned that there might be more chance of agreement if the details of legislation were left to a small group from each House, who, in various ways, might be induced to agree.

The decades preceding the Civil War were perhaps the period when conflict of interest between the House and Senate was most severe. It is no coincidence then that this was precisely the period in which the institutional arrangements for dealing with conflict of interest between the chambers acquired the practices that make the modern Congressional conference committee so powerful.

During the century following the Civil War the primary developments in the conference system were in the methods of control of the managers. The need for control was exemplified in the tariff bill of 1883 in which the party leaders used the conference committee to manipulate the House and the Senate into accepting higher tariff rates than either body would have been willing to accept if separate votes had been permitted. In reaction to maneuvers such as these, several pieces of machinery for control of the conference committee were introduced. Among these were (1) the provision adopted in 1902 by the House stating that before a conference report is considered it should be printed in the *Congressional Record* with a statement of explanation (except during the last six days of the session), and (2) a Senate rule, adopted in 1918, providing that conferees cannot insert matter not approved by either chamber nor strike matter approved by both chambers.

Such rules have probably strengthened the conference committee system because the introduction of explicit limitations on the conferees allowed the two chambers to employ the conference system with less fear that the system would be abused. Some of the specific controls that were imposed (such as the Senate rule of 1918) were attempts to limit the range of feasible agreements of the conferees to better approximate the range of dispute between the chambers.

The history of the Congressional conference committee illustrates how conflict of interest analysis might be used to shed light on certain aspects of the development of political institutions. From the origin of the conference in the fourteenth century in England, through the colonial legislatures, and from the earliest days of Congress, the conference has been a significant arena for bargaining over conflicts of interest between two legislative chambers. In the United States by the eve of the Civil War the procedures of the Congressional conference committee had developed to such an extent that the agreements of the conferees could almost be regarded as binding on the two chambers. The more recent arrangements for control of the conferees are largely designed to guarantee that the range of feasible conference agreements will not extend beyond the zone of disagreement between the chambers.

The conference system was employed by the English parliament, the American colonial legislatures, and the Congress because it was an efficient bargaining arena for the handling of differences arising out of conflicts of interest that were certain to exist between two legislative chambers. However, many other institutional arrangements are possible. In fact, when Temperley surveyed the bicameral legislatures of the world in 1910 he found that only Spain and Portugal shared with the United States a conference or joint committee system to resolve differences between two chambers.

The practices that gave the American conference system so much strength were developed in the period before the Civil War, the period that probably had the greatest conflict of interest between the House and Senate. The more recent methods of controlling the conferees are simply devices to guarantee that the interests that are not in conflict between the chambers do not enter the bargaining process of the conferees. Thus in a variety of ways the theoretical concept of conflict of interest in a bargaining game has some value in analyzing the historical development of an important political institution.

C. The Conference System as a Two-person Bargaining Game

As the conference system developed over six centuries, its activities tended to approximate more and more closely the model of the two-person bargaining game. The House and Senate conferees can now each be regarded as a unified actor; if the two sides reach an agreement, the agreement is practically certain to be accepted by both chambers. No agreement in conference is nearly always equivalent to no bill at all. Using this model, the conflict of interest can be readily determined from the utilities of the two sides, and appropriate forms of the general hypothesis can be formulated.

Behind this simple model is a series of assumptions that need to be examined individually. Of course, as in almost every model in the social sciences, the assumptions are oversimplifications of the situations they describe. The implicit claim made for such a model is only that there is an interesting range of cases for which the assumptions are sufficiently accurate to make the model a fruitful way of looking at the behavior in question.

The assumptions of the model can be regarded as applications of the definitions of the words "two-person bargaining game" in the context of the Congressional conference committee. Table 5-1 lists these assumptions together. The validity of these assumptions will now be examined in sequence, and then the history of the conference system will be reconsidered briefly as a progression toward the approximation of the two-person bargaining game model described by these assumptions. The next section will employ this model for a conflict of interest analysis of a case study of conference activity. (For an exposition of the procedures used in the modern Congressional conference committee this section draws upon Steiner, 1951, 7–11.)

I.A. Each Delegation of Conferees Is United. This assumption is never completely accurate, but it is an excellent approximation for at least some instances.

One factor promoting unity of the delegations is the norm that a conferee's first duty is to defend his house's interests, not his own. While exceptions are not hard to find, this principle remains the norm. An interesting illustration is Representative Curtis' explanation of two apparently contradictory actions: *signing* the conference report on Medicare (which he judged to be faithful to the House version) but voting *against* it on the floor. He said,

> It is important to explain the difference between the responsibility that a Member assumes as a conferee, the responsibilities as I see them in working out the differences between the House and Senate versions, and the responsibilities a Member has in his

TABLE 5-1
Assumptions of the Model of the
Congressional Conference Committee

I. Two-Person
  A. Each delegation of conferees is united.
  B. No outsiders participate in the conference.
II. Bargaining
  A. The two sides can communicate and make binding agreements.
  B. If no agreement is reached, a single predetermined outcome occurs, namely no bill.
III. Game
  A. Each side has utilities that are stable.
  B. Each side's utilities are known to the other side.
  C. Payoffs to each side are determined by the strategy choices of the players (in this case according to II.A and II.B).

---

primary capacity of representing his people. (*Congressional Record,* 1965, 18391)

The unity of the delegations is also promoted by the committee system in each chamber. A common theme in the literature on Congress is the high degree of integration in some of the standing committees. For example, Fenno (1963, 80), who defines integration as "the degree to which a committee is able to minimize conflict among its roles and subgroups, by heading off or resolving the conflicts that arise," finds that:

> Five important characteristics of the Appropriations Committee [of the House] which help explain Committee integration are (1) the existence of a well-articulated and deeply rooted consensus on Committee goals or tasks (2) the nature of the Committee's subject matter; (3) the legislative orientation of its members; (4) the attractiveness of the Committee for its members; and (5) the stability of Committee membership. (1963, 81)

A number of factors tend to make a conference delegation even better integrated than the standing legislative committee from which its members are chosen. The delegation is made up largely of senior committee members, and these senior members are ordinarily the ones who have done most of the work on the bill in question, have worked together on many bills, and have the largest stake in the norms that support committee integration. In addition, the chairman usually has some flexibility in choosing among the less senior members and he may use this flexibility to select a more cohesive group. Since each delegation votes as a unit within the conference, a minority viewpoint has little leverage, and the unity of the delegation is further enhanced.

I.B. No Outsiders Participate in the Conference. The point here is not that outsiders such as the President or the public do not matter— they do. The assumption is merely that outsiders cannot take an active part in the actual bargaining process. The validity of this assumption is supported by the secrecy with which conferences are conducted. In the judgment of Gross (1953, 323), "There are probably less [*sic*] 'leaks' from conference committees than any other brand of secret meeting in the nation's capital." Of course, the President and other executive officials often have a great stake in the decisions of a conference committee, and one of the conferees may provide them with good information on the bargaining process. Nevertheless, there is a norm among legislators that the conference is legislative business and that while the Executive Department can make its preferences known, any pressures it exerts at this stage are likely to be resented.

II.A. The Two Sides Can Communicate and Make Binding Agreements. Obviously the two sides can communicate freely in the committee. Furthermore, there exists a common basis of experience so that the two sides can easily understand (even though not necessarily agree with) each other. The coding problem of how to interpret the actors' words in terms of strategic choices in the bargaining model has to be dealt with on a case-by-case basis (see also Chapter 4).

The conferees cannot formally bind their respective chambers to acceptance of their report, but usually they can almost guarantee its acceptance. This power is supported by the conferees' tactical position as the ones who can claim to know most about what the other chamber can and cannot be made to agree to. It is further enhanced by the rule in both chambers that it is not in order to amend a conference report, but that it must be accepted or rejected as a whole. Gross sums up the strength of the conferees' ability to make binding agreements by quoting Galloway's statement (1946, 99) from Senator George Norris: "Every experienced legislator knows that it is the hardest thing in the world to defeat a conference report."

II.B. If No Agreement Is Reached a Single Predetermined Outcome Occurs, Namely No Bill. This assumption seems trivial, but it is not strictly accurate. The conference committee can write a partial report and the two chambers can each decide what they wish to do about the items remaining in dispute. Also, the rules of the House of Representatives permit the appointment of new conferees if no report is issued after a specified length of time. Furthermore, on many issues the length of time required to reach an agreement also matters. This is a problem that will be dealt with explicitly in the analysis of the case study.

III.A. The Two Sides Have Utility Schedules that Are Stable. While it is true that the preferences of the conferees may change somewhat during the bargaining process, for the most part these preferences are well-established by the time the bill goes to conference. By that time the bill has gone through the complete legislative committee process and has been dealt with by the full chamber. The conferees have undoubtedly been active in this process, and at the late stage of the conference committee are likely to have very clear ideas about what is important in the bill and what has only marginal value. Thus it can usually be assumed that during the conference meetings the participants do not learn anything that would alter their preferences.

III.B. Each Side's Utilities Are Known to the Other Side. The Senate conferees are likely to know a good deal about what the House conferees would like the conference report to say, and vice versa. The early stages of the conference probably provide both sides with further information about the other's preferences.

III.C. Payoffs to Each Side Are Determined by the Strategy Choices of the Players (in This Case According to the Definition of the Bargaining Game in II.A and II.B). This assumption is part of the definition of a game. Its specific content for the conference committee is given in the two assumptions which describe the particular kind of game in use, namely the bargaining game.

The history of the Congressional conference committee as an institution can be regarded as a progression toward fulfilling these assumptions of the two-person bargaining game. The strategic interaction of the conference could always have been regarded as a game (thus fulfilling assumptions III.A, III.B and III.C), and there is little evidence as to whether the two sides were always as well-unified as they are now (assumption I.A). However, while the British conference system was superseded in the eighteenth century by the development of a strong cabinet system (thus violating assumption I.B—no outside participation), the American conference committee developed along the lines of a largely autonomous institution within the framework of the system of standing legislative committees. As the Congressional conference committee demonstrated its value, it was granted more and more privileges, especially in the period just before the Civil War. These privileges slowly became consolidated into firm precedents, so that the contemporary Congressional conference committee is so strong that its agreements are usually equivalent to binding commitments on the chambers (assumption II.A). Now that the conference committee is well-established as the institution through which differences on a bill are worked out between the two chambers of Congress, failure to reach an agreement in conference is almost tantamount to a failure of Congress to pass any version of the bill (assumption II.B).

D. The Appropriations Controversy of 1962

THE CASE STUDY APPROACH

The functioning of the Congressional conference committee approximates the assumptions of the two-person bargaining game model. To the extent that the assumptions of this model are fulfilled, an analysis of actual conference activity in terms of conflict of interest is possible using the tools developed in Part I of this study. A fruitful way to demonstrate a political application of these tools is to apply them to a specific case of conference activity. Such a demonstration is the purpose of this section.

The demonstration should be helpful in suggesting a variety of factors that would have to be dealt with by a fully adequate theory of conflict of interest. It might also be helpful in illustrating the kind of insights into a complex bargaining process that can be derived from the theory of conflict of interest, even in its present early state.

One difficulty in studying the modern conference system, however, is that the system works so well that an agreement is reached on almost every bill. For instance, of the 1004 public laws sent to conference in the twenty-two years of the 70th through 80th Congresses (1927–1948), only 31 died in conference for lack of an agreement (Steiner, 1951, 177).

This very low rate of failure can be explained in large part by pointing out that failure to reach an agreement in conference reflects badly upon the conferees. Such a personal cost of failure makes the no agreement point for the conferees substantially lower than would be indicated by a consideration of only the policy issues at stake. As indicated in Chapter 2, a lowering of the no agreement point never raises and nearly always lowers the (relative) conflict of interest. Even with large stakes and high absolute conflict of interest, if there is a low amount of relative conflict of interest a low rate of failure is predicted. In this way, conflict of interest analysis helps explain the low rate of failure of the conference system over the long run.

This still leaves the question: what kind of case study should be selected for analysis? It would be all too easy to select a typical case in which the assumptions of the two-person bargaining game model are fulfilled, some differences exist between the two chambers, the conflict of interest is low, and, as usual, a compromise is reached with only routine haggling. Such a case study would be of little value in demonstrating the contributions or limitations of a conflict of interest analysis.

A more valuable case would be one that challenged the assumptions of the simple bargaining game model, and that exhibited a great deal of conflictful behavior. Such a complex case would be deviant rather than typical, but its value would derive from its very deviation. By its very complexity it would serve to demonstrate both the range of problems that can be treated with the present set of tools for conflict of interest analysis, and the limitations of these tools.

An excellent example is the unusually bitter Congressional appropriations dispute of 1962. Before it was over, four different issues were intertwined in the controversy, and although no bill died in conference many government agencies almost ran out of money.

CHRONOLOGY OF THE DISPUTE

The present treatment of the dispute takes its description of the events from Pressman (1966, 3–6). First some background information is necessary to understand the issues at stake.

> The Constitution, I(7), requires that "All bills for raising revenue shall originate in the House of Representatives." By tradition, this has been true of appropriations bills also. Appropriations bills originate in one of the twelve subcommittees of the fifty-member House Appropriations Committee and recommendations are usually accepted without change by the full House. After House passage, each bill is referred to the Senate Appropriations Committee, which consists of twenty-seven members and thirteen subcommittees. The Senate subcommittees hold brief hearings, and the House-approved funds are usually increased in the Senate. Following Senate passage, the bill goes to conference—historically held on the Senate side of the Capitol and presided over by a Senate conferee. The final amount adopted is usually a compromise between Senate and House figures.

> If appropriations legislation for the new fiscal year has not been completed by July 1, it is necessary for the two houses to adopt some kind of emergency legislation to enable the government agencies to continue operations on a daily basis. This is usually done by joint resolution.   (Pressman, 1966, 2)

The course of the dispute is summarized in Table 5-2.

The outcomes on each of the four issues are described by Fenno (1966, 640–641). The *meeting place* of the conferences on appropriations (Issue 1) now takes place in a room which straddles the center line of the Capitol rather than in one on the Senate side as before. The Senate continues to accept the *House prerogative to originate all appropriations bills* (Issue 2), although the Senate may at any time reassert its claims to equality in this regard. A temporary solution was negotiated on the third issue. This solution provided that, instead of always being a Senator, the *chairman of a conference* would be selected by the two subcommittees dealing with each bill. Although a joint committee was set up to find a permanent solution to the chairmanship issue, this committee has never met and apparently never will. As is so often the case in bargaining, a "temporary" solution became accepted as permanent. The fourth issue, *size of appropriations,* has to be resolved anew for each new appropriations bill. As long as

TABLE 5-2

Event	Issue	Date
House Appropriations Committee asks for rotation between House and Senate side of the Capitol as sites for conferences on appropriations bills.	1. Meeting place	April 1962
Senate counters with proposal that it originate half of all appropriations bills.	2. Origination of appropriations bills	
Appropriations are held up because no conference meets until July.	1 and 2	through July
House passes supplemental appropriations bill.		June 14
Hayden (Chmn., Sen. Appr. Comm.) offers to meet in Old Supreme Court Chamber, halfway between the House and Senate.	1 Solved	
Cannon (Chmn., House Appr. Comm.) asks that a House member be chairman half the time.	3. Chairman of conference	
Senate passes supplemental appropriations bill with more generous terms than House. (Rep. Cannon has said higher figures show that the Senators are profligate spenders.)	4. Size of appropriations	June 23
Mansfield (Sen. Maj. Leader) calls for examination of the whole question of conferences because of the dangerous implications of a delay in appropriations.	1, 2, 3, 4	
House passes a continuing resolution providing for continuation of old projects, but not new ones.	4	June 28
Teams of negotiators from the two Appropriations Committees try to resolve the dispute.	2, 3, 4	July
A temporary solution reached which provides that for the rest of the session the chairmen will be selected by the subcommittees dealing with each bill, and a joint committee will be set up to consider disputed issues.	3 Temporarily solved	July 18
Senate passes a continuing appropriations bill for Agriculture, after a deadlock with the House over Agricultural research funds.	4	Oct. 4
House asserts Senate cannot initiate an appropriations bill, and Senate asserts that it can.	2	
Cannon blocks the sending to conference of the Supplemental Appropriations Bill to discourage Senate from adding money to House appropriations bills.	4	Oct. 12

the other issues are not opened up again the money question can be compromised with relatively little difficulty.

ANALYSIS OF THE DISPUTE

Six features of this dispute will now be examined to see what they can contribute to the theory of conflict of interest as well as to the study of the Congressional conference committee:

1. The importance of prestige considerations,
2. The immediate relevance of money,
3. Time as an element in the bargaining process,
4. The compounding of issues during the dispute,
5. Long vs. short term issues,
6. Relationships between chambers, issues, and parties.

1. *Prestige.* Conflict of interest is especially high on issues involving prestige if there are no feasible agreements which allow both sides to be well satisfied. In other words, bargaining over issues of prestige, symbols, status, and so forth can readily involve relatively incompatible goals.

The demand by the Senate to originate one-half of all appropriations bills (Issue 2 in the chronology) illustrates the nature of this problem. One feasible agreement might have been that the Senate would be allowed to originate one-quarter of all such bills (rather than none as the House insisted or half as the Senate asked). However, such an agreement would be poor for both sides because it would require the Senate to give up its claim to equality in the appropriations process, and it would require the House to give up its longstanding prerogative to be the sole initiator of appropriations bills. Although more was at stake in this issue than prestige, the fact that both sides based their positions on high principles like "equality" and "constitutionality" meant that it would be difficult to invent a compromise that was reasonably satisfactory to both sides. No such compromise was invented, the conflict of interest remained high, and no agreement was reached in this issue.

2. *Money.* Bargaining over the allocation of money may result in a game with conflict of interest of $\frac{1}{2}$ as in the split-the-dollar game (Figure 5-1). The issue of the overall magnitude of the appropriations (number 4 in the chronology) may have had a region of feasible agreements much like the split-the-dollar game and hence conflict of interest might have been roughly one-half on this issue.

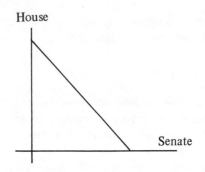

FIGURE 5-1.   A Split-the-Dollar
Bargaining Game

Much more likely, however, the range of disagreement over money was not that great in 1962.   Either side would probably have preferred the other's dollar amount rather than cause the disaster of providing no appropriations or an extremely long delay.   For this reason the bargaining over the allocation of money probably had a relatively narrow range of disagreement and thus low conflict of interest on this issue, as shown in Figure 5-2.

Thus conflict of interest over money can be either high or low depending upon how each side views the other's proposal relative to the no agreement point and its own proposal.   Using this criterion one could expect that during the Cold War the appropriations process for the Defense Department would have had little conflict of interest in the conference committee.   In contrast to Defense appropriations, bargaining between the two chambers of Congress for themselves might be similar to the split-the-dollar game because the conflict of interest

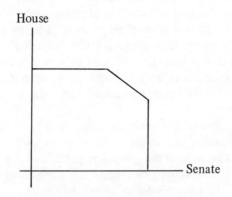

FIGURE 5-2.   Low Conflict of Interest

of the chambers might be great on such an issue. These conjectures are confirmed by Pressman (1966, 61):

> Some subcommittee sets (like Defense) are well-known for the cordiality prevailing between Senate and House groups, while others (like Legislative Appropriations) have often been the focal points for severe conflict.

Not only can similar preferences lead to low conflict of interest over money (as in Defense), but so can the possibility of vote-trading. If one chamber is very concerned about one kind of expenditure and the other is highly concerned with another, then a quite satisfactory and feasible agreement would be for each to accept the other's preferred program. Thus vote-trading can lower conflict of interest on issues which would otherwise have high conflict of interest.

Money issues need not have the large conflict of interest associated with split-the-dollar games if the range of disagreement is small relative to the resultant harm if no agreement is reached or if vote-trading between different issues is feasible. In the 1962 dispute over appropriations, a delayed agreement meant significant disruption in federal programs and knowledge of this tended to lower the conflict of interest between House and Senate conferees by lowering the null point.

3. *Time.* The amount of disruption obviously depends on the length of the delay. This complicates the model of the bargaining process because there is no fixed payoff to each side if agreement is not reached. Instead, the null point depends upon the length of time the two sides continue without an agreement. Indeed the lack of a unique null point violates assumption II.B, and means that conflict of interest is not definable for the appropriations dispute in terms of the familiar two-person bargaining game model.

Of course this complication—the null point's being dependent on the length of time it takes to reach an agreement—is not unique to conference committee activity. It appears in a wide variety of bargaining processes such as negotiations during a war. Perhaps the most obvious and common example is union-management bargaining in which the costs to both sides of not reaching an agreement mount daily during a strike.

Because a unique null point does not exist, conflict of interest cannot be measured as it could be for a bargaining game. This is so because the conflict of interest in the bargaining game depends in part on the location of the null point. Nevertheless, some aspects of the situation can still be readily analyzed in terms of conflict of interest.   Clearly the conflict of interest can be calculated with respect to any given null point.   For example, if passage of any appropriations were delayed one week beyond the start of the fiscal year a given null point would result.   This point could then be used in the calculation of the conflict of interest between the House and the Senate conferees with respect to a delay of one week.   This is restricted conflict of interest in the sense that it measures the conflict of interest in the game when the null point is associated with a one-week delay.   The restricted conflict of interest could also be calculated for a two-week delay, a three-week delay, and so on.

Another approach to the question of how to handle the variable null point is to note that a delay affects not only the null point, but every feasible agreement as well.   This is true because the costs of disruption resulting from a delay in appropriations (for example) can never be completely made up.   Thus as time goes on every feasible agreement moves downward and to the left in the graph of the game (see Figure 5-3).   If all points move at the same rate (as well they might), then the shape of the region of feasible agreements remains unchanged and the null point stays in the same relative position in this region.   In that case, the restricted conflict of interest remains exactly the same no matter what the delay.

4. *Compounding of Issues.*   One of the most interesting features of the appropriations dispute of 1962 was the way in which issues became compounded.   First the House raised the issue of where appropriations conferences should be held, and then the Senate countered with the issue of who may originate appropriations bills.   The first issue was then resolved by a compromise offer by Senator Hayden,

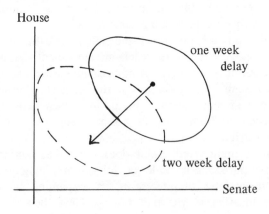

FIGURE 5-3.   The Effects of Delay

but then Rep. Cannon raised a third issue by asking that a House member chair the conference half the time.   Then in June the Senate and the House passed different interim appropriations measures which brought into the open the fourth issue, the size of appropriations.   In July a temporary solution was negotiated on the second issue.   Things were quiet until October when the fourth issue again arose over the size of appropriations for the Agriculture Department, and the procedure used by the Senate caused the House to return to the second issue and repeat its assertions that the Senate could not initiate an appropriations measure.

It is clear from this case history that new issues can be brought into an ongoing dispute either as a deliberate tactic by one side to improve its bargaining position by expanding the range of feasible agreements, or by normal functioning of the institutions that can force issues to the forefront even if neither side wishes to deal with them immediately.   The issue of whether the Senate can originate appropriations bills illustrates both these possibilities.   The first time this issue was raised by the Senate it was obviously done to help counter the House's demand to change the precedent on the location of the appropriations conferences.   However, the second time the issue of origination was raised it was by the House in October as a response to the Senate's procedural action on a continuing appropriations bill.

The effect of compounding one issue by joining another issue to it is to require that the dispute will be completely settled only if an agreement is reached which deals with both issues.   Of course, the issues may later be disconnected and settled one at a time (as was done in 1962 when the first issue was settled by a compromise and the second was later dropped), but if the dispute is to be completely resolved agreement has to deal with each outstanding issue.   The effect of compounding the bargaining process by raising a new issue (or issues) is to expand the region of feasible agreements to include agreement on all the issues at once.   This expansion of the region of feasible agreements can be expected to increase the stakes of the bargaining process.   However, as was shown in Chapter 2, the conflict of interest can either increase or decrease after such an expansion depending on how the new feasible outcomes are regarded by the two sides.   In the case of adding the issue of who can originate appropriations bills, the resulting expansion of the region of feasible agreements probably increased the conflict of interest by adding possibilities that the Senate strongly preferred but that the House did not find at all desirable.   An example of how this expansion might have looked is shown in Figures 5-4 and 5-5, neither of which is normalized.   The conflict of

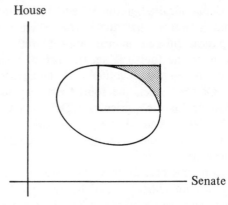

FIGURE 5-4.   Before New Issue

interest in each figure is the ratio of the shaded area to the rectangle, and the conflict of interest is greater in Figure 5-5 due to the expansion.

5. *Long vs. Short Term Issues.*   In the case of the appropriation dispute of 1962, the four issues that were compounded included both long and short term issues.   The procedural issues of meeting place, origination of bills, and chairmanship were all long term issues touching on precedents dating as far back as the first session of Congress.   Any change in these precedents could easily alter the Congressional procedures for decades to come.   The short term issue was the magnitude of the appropriations for fiscal year 1963, an issue of no small importance in itself.   The short and long term issues were closely bound together because the cost of an active dispute on the long term issues

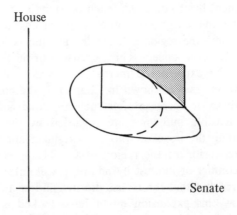

FIGURE 5-5.   After New Issue

was a failure to pass an appropriations bill (the short term issue), and the cost of such a failure could be seen to rise week by week.

A number of comparisons can be made between long and short term issues with respect to their conflict of interest. First of all, there is the question of future negotiations. As Pressman (1966, 70f.) points out, Schelling (1960) makes the point that the expectation of an issue arising again can lead both sides to maintain an image of firmness. But an opposite effect is also sometimes found because the prospect of future negotiations may allow the participants to invent feasible agreements (involving promises of future action) which can reconcile otherwise incompatible goals. Another difference is that the payoffs for the settlement of long term issues are usually much more dependent upon the time horizon of the participants than are the immediate payoffs which flow from settlement of a short term issue.

The distinction between long and short term issues must be made within the context of the bargaining process itself, and it is tenuous at best. An issue that appears to be long term, such as who shall chair the conference committee, might be settled by a temporary solution and thus take on some of the characteristics of a short term issue. On the other hand, a short term issue, like the magnitude of the appropriations for fiscal year 1963, is in an important sense just one stage in the long term struggle between the House and the Senate over financial policy for the Federal Government.

6. *Chambers, Issues, and Parties.* The conflict of interest between the House and Senate conferees in the 1962 appropriations dispute was largely a result of the institutional differences between the two chambers. It is hardly coincidental that the Chairman of the *House* Appropriations Committee advocated that the appropriations conferences should no longer be held solely on the Senate side of the Capitol; that the House retain the sole right to initiate appropriations bills; and that the chairman of the conference should no longer always be a Senator. Nor is it coincidental that the Chairman of the *Senate* Appropriations Committee took the opposite position on these issues. Even differential preferences for the size of appropriations may be influenced by institutional factors that usually lead the House to be less generous than the Senate in providing appropriations (Fenno, 1966).

A Congressman's preferences on the four issues of the appropriations dispute of 1962 were affected by whether that Congressman was a Senator or a Representative. The partial correspondence between preferences on issues and chamber membership helps to account for the conflict of interest between the two teams of men who negotiated on these issues.   However, the conflict of interest between these two teams was reduced by the fact that the chairman and a majority of each team were all members of the same political party (the Democratic Party) and hence had certain partisan interests in common.   These relationships can be thought of as an overlapping cleavage between issue preference and chamber membership and a crosscutting cleavage between chambers and parties.

In general, overlapping cleavages increase conflict of interest and crosscutting cleavages reduce conflict of interest.   For present purposes it is sufficient to point out that the appropriations dispute of 1962 provides an example of this proposition.   A full treatment of the relationship between cleavages and conflict of interest, including a derivation of this proposition, is given in Chapter 7 on societal conflict of interest.

ANOTHER LOOK AT THE THEORY OF CONFLICT OF INTEREST

This discussion of six features of the appropriations dispute of 1962 suggests a variety of factors which would have to be dealt with by a fully adequate theory of conflict of interest.   These factors are: (a) the manner in which vote trading changes the bargaining process; (b) the meaning of conflict of interest when the null point is not fixed; (c) the precise way in which issues are joined together in a compound bargaining process; (d) the variety of differences between long and short term issues; and (e) the way in which overlapping and crosscutting cleavages affect conflict of interest.   A few thoughts have already been offered about how the simple bargaining game model might be enhanced to deal with most of these items, and some preliminary indications of what the results for conflict of interest might be have been noted.   Without doubt the case study method has been helpful in suggesting directions for expansion of the theory of conflict of interest.

The case study of the 1962 appropriations dispute has also shown that a number of insights into a complex bargaining process can be derived from the theory of conflict of interest even in its present early state.   Among the topics that the current theory was able to analyze with some cogency are: (a) the conditions under which prestige considerations increase conflict of interest; (b) some special factors that can be used to determine whether conflict of interest over money issues will be high or low; (c) the way in which the effect of a given delay in reaching an agreement can be analyzed; (d) the reason conflict of interest is likely to increase if one side adds a new issue just to improve its bargaining position; (e) several ways in which conflict of interest is dependent on whether the issue is long term or short term; and (f) some ways in which institutional and partisan differences can raise or lower conflict of interest.

Often one of the main problems in understanding a political institution is the lack of a framework in which to think about what is happening. This chapter has shown that an analysis in terms of conflict of interest can provide such a framework for studying certain historical trends, for examining and predicting the intensity of conflictful behavior, and for explaining various aspects of the bargaining process. Because the Congressional conference committee comes so close to fulfilling the definition of a simple two-actor bargaining game, future work on the conference committee may yield not only a better understanding of Congress, but also a better understanding of political bargaining in general.

E. Appendix: Possible Statistical Tests

THE MEANING OF A TEST

A theory of conflict of interest can be used to help analyze past events in order to better understand them. This is the way in which the theory has been applied to the examination of the history of the Congressional conference committee and the analysis of the appropriations dispute of 1962.

A theory of conflict of interest can also be used to make predictions. In order to do this, the way in which the general hypothesis applies to the Congressional conference committee must be specified so that a particular theory is formulated. Used in this way, the theory is falsifiable because the predictions may turn out to be wrong. In this sense, the theory can be tested. This appendix provides an example of one way in which the theory of conflict of interest can be tested. The example describes procedures that can be applied to the study of the Congressional conference committee. While these procedures are feasible, they have not actually been carried out in this study.

CALCULATION OF CONFLICT OF INTEREST

The model that provides the context for this example is the two-person bargaining game as has already been discussed earlier in this chapter. Although some episodes of conference activity clearly do not fit this simple model very well (e.g., the 1962 appropriations dispute), the consideration of most bills can be reasonably approximated by the elementary model.

In order to determine how much conflict of interest there is between the two teams of conferees on a given bill, the utilities of each side for the various feasible agreements must be determined.   Plotting these points gives the region of feasible agreements, and determining this region along with the point representing no agreement permits measurement of conflict of interest.

The problem that immediately arises is the apparent need to examine one by one the vast number of possible versions of the bill which might be agreed upon by the two sides.   One way in which this problem can be dealt with has already been described in Chapter 4, where it was noted that measurement of only three or four possible outcomes may be sufficient to provide a good approximation of the amount of conflict of interest present.   In the case of the conference committee, another approach to the measurement problem is available.

This other approach uses the fact that while there may be literally thousands of different feasible agreements on how to reconcile the differences between the House and Senate bills, there are usually only a very limited number of differences between the bills.   If the possibility of creatively reformulating the differences is put aside, the total agreements can be regarded as combinations of agreements on each of the separate differences.   These differences can be called "clauses." Then, for example, if there are ten clauses in dispute and even if there are only two ways of resolving each clause, there are 2^{10} or 1024 possible elementary agreements in the region of feasible outcomes. However, all that actually needs to be determined is the upper-right-hand boundary of the region, not the entire region.   If there are ten clauses in dispute, there are only eleven (i.e., $10 + 1$) feasible agreements on this boundary.

To see why this is so, consider each of the clauses separately, and suppose that each side wants to have its own way on each clause, but that not all the clauses are of equal importance.   Suppose a number between 0 and 10 could be assigned to each clause representing its utility to the House conferees, and another such number for the Senate conferees.   Table 5-3 gives an example of a set of such numbers, along with the ease to the House of being generous to the Senate in letting the Senate have its way on a given clause.   The ease of being generous for each clause is, by definition, the ratio of its utility to the Senate divided by its utility to the House (see also Chapter 1).

These numbers are almost sufficient to determine how much con-

TABLE 5-3
Example of Preferences on Clauses,
Arranged by Ease of Being Generous

Clause	Utility to Senate Team	Utility to House Team	Ease of Generosity of House to Senate
A	10	2	5
B	4	1	4
C	7	3	2.33
D	6	3	2
E	5	4	1.25
F	3	3	1
G	5	5	1
H	2	8	.25
I	1	4	.25
J	1	5	.20

flict of interest there is, even though there are more than 1000 possible agreements. All that needs to be added is the utility to each side of the other's original version of the bill (taken relative to no bill as the zero and that side's original version as the unit). With this information, the upper-right-hand boundary of the region of feasible agreements can be plotted and the conflict of interest determined (see Figure 5-6).[1]

MEASUREMENT OF UTILITIES

The advantage in calculating conflict of interest in terms of the importance of separate clauses is that the necessary information may be relatively easy to get from informed sources. The sources might be the conferees themselves, members of their committee staffs, or selected officials in the Executive Department.

The appropriate questions could take a form similar to the follow-

---

[1] The boundary is determined by first plotting the House bill, then plotting the agreement which represents the House's giving in on the clause for which its ease of generosity is the highest. The other points along the boundary are derived in sequence by having the House give in on clause after clause in order of decreasing ease of generosity. The last bill on the boundary is the Senate's original bill.

The process can be performed algebraically as well as geometrically, and the formula is long but straightforward.

The calculation of conflict of interest using clauses assumes the utilities for separate clauses are linear additive, and that there are no nonlinear compromises within or between clauses. The method is not too sensitive to partial failures in these assumptions, but if either is grossly inaccurate then the direct method of calculation or the few point approximation of if would have to be used.

House

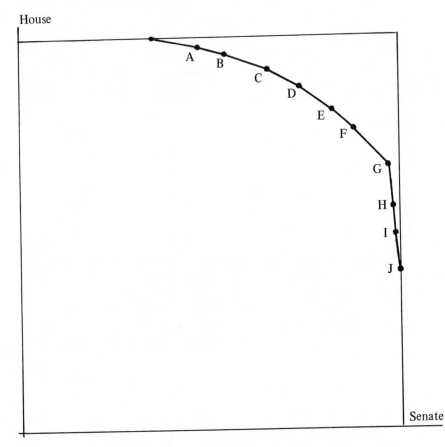

FIGURE 5-6. Normalized Bargaining Game
(Based on Table 5-1, with extra data that the House regards the
Senate's original bill as four tenths of the way from no bill to the
House bill, and the Senate regards the House bill as three-tenths of
the way from no bill to the Senate bill. Points are labeled with the
most recent clause the House would give the Senate.)

ing: "How important is it to you as a Senate conferee to have this
clause resolved in the Senate's favor? Say zero points means it does
not matter at all, and ten points means that having your way on this
clause is of utmost importance. How important is this clause?" Assuming that the answers had cardinal significance between clauses on
the same bill (which may be roughly the case), the answers to this
question would give the numbers needed to fill in Table 5-3.

This question has to be asked of the Senate and of the House conferees on each disputed clause of every bill to be studied.   The information should be gathered after both chambers have finished formulating their own version of the bill, but before the conference has actually begun, so as not to rely on the assumption of stable preferences.

Alternative techniques to interviewing are available to measure utilities of the conferees.   Among the sources of information that might be used to construct utility schedules are content analysis of speeches, the voting record in each chamber on the individual clauses in dispute, and objective differences in the chambers such as differential representation of special interests or party control.

As a very simple example of the use of the clause approach to measurement of conflict of interest, suppose the House team cares most about the disputed clauses that the Senate team cares least about, and vice versa. Then the region of feasible agreements bulges and there is little conflict of interest.   On the other hand, if the disputed things one side wants most are the same things the other side cares most about, then the boundary of the region is flat and there tends to be high conflict of interest.   The virtue of a formal way to calculate conflict of interest is that it can be much more precise than this and can distinguish not only between the extreme cases, but also among the intermediate cases.   It takes into account not only the comparative preferences of the individual clauses in the dispute, but also the costs of failure to reach an agreement, and the preferences of each side for the other's original version of the bill.

HYPOTHESES

The general hypothesis is that other things being equal, the more conflict of interest there is, the more conflictful behavior.   As always, conflict of interest means relative conflict of interest unless otherwise specified.   An alternative hypothesis that should also be tested is that the more *absolute* conflict of interest there is, the more conflictful behavior.   Absolute conflict of interest as defined in Chapter 4 depends only on the extent of the conflicting interests and does not take into account the extent of the common interest.   The latter might be expected to reduce the likelihood of conflictful behavior.

Conflict of interest is calculated from the utilities of the participants for the feasible agreements and the no agreement point, and these utilities can be measured from interviews or by other means.   The other variable in the general hypothesis is conflictful behavior.

Conflictful behavior in the arena of the Congressional conference committee can take a variety of forms, and can be measured by a variety of indicators. Among these forms and indicators are:

1. Bill died in conference (i.e., no agreement was reached),
2. Compromise bill rejected by one or both chambers (indicating the compromise was not actually a feasible agreement),
3. Conference report did not settle all the outstanding issues, so that another conference was needed, and
4. Difficulty existed in the conference in reaching an agreement (as measurable by such things as the number of sessions needed and the length of committee meetings held).

Depending on how much data were available these indicators of conflictful behavior could be tested individually for their dependence on conflict of interest, or they could be combined into a composite measure of conflictful behavior and tested all at once. In either case conflict of interest and conflictful behavior would probably have to be measured for at least several dozen bills in order to test whether each prediction had sufficient statistical power to be able to determine whether the hypothesized relationship exists and, if it does, what the approximate strength of the relationship is.

As a supplement to the formal statistical test, the usefulness of such a theory can be evaluated by eliciting predictions from the people who were interviewed. The accuracy of the observers' predictions could later be compared to the accuracy of the prediction of the theory of conflict of interest. A close observer of conference activity, such as a staff member of a legislative committee, can use a wide variety of information in making his predictions. His advantages include familiarity with his side's preferences and with the personalities of the conferees; the recent history of relationships between the two chambers; executive pressures; and whatever idiosyncrasies may be relevant to this particular bill. On the other hand, the theoretical predictions are based on a theory which uses a model of the two-person bargaining game and the single explanatory variable of conflict of interest. A comparison of the accuracy of the theoretical predictions (using estimates of utilities supplied by, say, staff members) with the accuracy of the predictions of the staff members themselves, would provide an interesting indication of the degree of success of such a theory of conflict of interest in the arena of the Congressional conference committee.

6

Multilevel Decisionmaking in Bureaucracy

A. The Policy Formation Process

PURPOSES OF THIS CHAPTER

This chapter has three purposes: to present a multilevel model of bargaining in bureaucracies, to show how the theoretical concepts developed in Part I can be applied to the analysis of a model with an institutional setting, and to suggest some new questions that may prove useful in the study of how bureaucracies determine policy. The chapter begins with an examination of the role of bargaining in bureaucracy. Then a model is proposed to deal with the bargaining relationships between officials, focusing on the movement of issues from one level of the bureaucracy to another. The model is employed as a framework in which a conflict of interest analysis can be performed on the multilevel decisionmaking process in bureaucracy.

BARGAINING IN BUREAUCRACY

Bureaucracies are sometimes viewed as being monolithic organizations rationally pursuing a single goal. Thus for example, the economic theory of the firm assumes away differences in either goals or perceptions within an organization, as pointed out by March and Simon (1958, 124). Many authors have in recent years questioned assumptions of this kind, saying that bureaucracies *can not* be like that (i.e., complete rationality is impossible because of the complexity of the organization's environment); bureaucracies *are not* like that (i.e., differences within an organization on goals and perceptions do exist); and bureaucracies *should not* try to be like that (i.e., it is not efficient to try to run an organization as a monolith pursuing a single goal). Among the factors inhibiting complete rationality in an organization are the limitations in time, information and computing ability, which are treated by K. Deutsch (1963); personality factors (Lasswell, 1930); and interpersonal relationships (Argyris, 1960, 1962).

If an organization cannot be both monolithic and rational, perhaps it can achieve rationality by decomposing its problems and assigning different subproblems to different parts of the bureaucracy. Hitch and McKean (1960, 396–402) demonstrate that if the decomposition can be done perfectly in the sense that there are no interaction effects between the subproblems, then the optimizing of the subproblems yields an optimizing for the entire organization. Huntington (1961) and Tullock (1965) both find that organizations do in fact try to decompose their problems into independent subproblems, but that they can rarely be completely successful. Few decisionmaking problems can be so neatly divided up that their parts can be successfully dealt with in isolation.

If the decomposition of problems nearly always involves some interaction between the subproblems, a useful way to attain a degree of coordination between the subproblems is to let the separate parts of the bureaucracy that deal with the separate subproblems bargain with each other. Huntington (1961), Snyder, Bruck and Sapin (1962), and Wildavsky (1964) all find that this is precisely what happens in bureaucracies. Lindblom (1965), who calls this process "partisan mutual adjustment," argues that it can and does yield a satisfactory level of coordination.

This raises the question of why bargaining in bureaucracies does not appear as ubiquitous as this review suggests it in fact is. Several possible answers are suggested by March and Simon (1958, 131): bargaining places strains on the status and power systems in an organization and it legitimizes heterogeneity of goals in the organization. Therefore, they predict "almost all disputes in the organization will be defined as problems in analysis . . . and that bargaining (when it occurs) will frequently be concealed within an analytic framework."

March and Simon (1958, 129f.) also make useful distinctions

between four kinds of processes in organizations: problem-solving, persuasion, bargaining, and "politics." In the case of problem-solving, it is assumed that all participants have the same goals and the decision-problem is to find a solution that satisfies these criteria. In the case of persuasion, the individual goals differ, but are not taken as fixed. Bargaining takes the goals as fixed and agreement without persuasion is sought. By "politics" March and Simon mean a situation like bargaining except that the arena is not taken as fixed by the participants.

In the terms of the present study, problem-solving has no conflict of interest and persuasion is an attempt to lower the amount of conflict of interest, while bargaining and "politics" are processes aimed at reaching agreement in the presence of conflict of interest. This chapter deals with both bargaining at a given level of the organization and the "politics" of broadening the arena of decisionmaking. Because the last two processes are so closely linked, the term "bargaining" will be used to refer to both.

Bargaining in bureaucracies is not a simple matter of resolving disputes over subgoals and thereby reaching an optimal decision. Cyert and March (1963) provide a number of useful observations on how the bargaining in organizations (business firms in their case) actually proceeds. The organization's subgoals are often treated as a series of independent constraints. The subgoals are assigned to sub-units of the organization, and the subunits employ "acceptable-level decision rules" in dealing with them. The organization itself resolves incompatibilities between the different goals, partly by attending to different goals at different times.

This still leaves open the question of how the upper levels of the organization supervise the subunits. In talking about the President of the United States (and by extension a high official in any large bureaucracy) Neustadt (1960, 155) notes that time is the critical constraint governing the supervisory tactics used by the President. "A President's priorities are set not by the relative importance of a task, but by the relative necessity for him to do it. He deals first with things that are required of *him* next." This suggests that a superior might tend to accept any decision agreed upon by the different parts of the bureaucracy assigned to deal with the subproblems involved in the decision, and worry only about the issues on which the subordinates cannot agree.

Downs (1967, 147) criticizes this strategy because it gives the subordinates control over all matters on which they can agree. However, as he notes elsewhere, officials tend to be biased in favor of policies that advance interests associated with their own part of the bureaucracy. Since different parts of the bureaucracy are assigned different subgoals, the superiors are often justified in assuming that if the biased subordinates can resolve an issue among themselves then the different parts of the problem have already been coordinated to some (perhaps very limited) extent. Thus despite the serious drawbacks of such a strategy, it does have the advantage of conserving the superior's time so he can deal with those problems that *he* must deal with, including those the subordinates could not resolve among themselves.

B. The Bargaining Stages

CABLE-CLEARING PROCESS

To help deal with these aspects of bargaining in bureaucracies a particular example of the policy formation process will be considered. The example is the cable-clearing process in Washington whereby a cable sent by one agency giving instructions to its representatives abroad must often be cleared with other agencies that are also concerned with the cable's content. The model to be developed applies to a wide range of bureaucratic activity; the cable-clearing process is chosen merely as a concrete point of departure.

To be even more specific, suppose the Department of Defense wishes to send instructions to its representative at a NATO military planning conference. The Defense Department will probably have to get the approval of the State Department before sending the cable, since political issues are likely to be involved. Of course the Secretary of Defense will not discuss every such cable with the Secretary of State. Instead, the Secretaries employ management by exception. The Secretaries let appropriate subordinates in their two departments consider the issue. If the subordinates can reach an agreement on the message the cable can be sent, but otherwise the issue may indeed have to be considered by the two Secretaries. If even the Secretaries cannot agree, the President will have to decide the issue.

This highly simplified description of the cable-clearing process suggests a model of the policy formation process. This model, in its simplest form, consists of the President, and officials of two agencies (or departments, bureaus, etc.), each with an upper level and a lower level, for a total of five people. (See the simplified organization chart in Figure 6-1. For a mathematical theory of organization charts, see Starbuck, 1965). The rules of the strategic interaction are quite straightforward. If the lower levels of the two agencies can

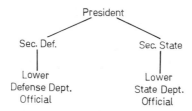

FIGURE 6-1. Organization
Chart of a Simple
Bureaucracy

agree on a cable, that is the cable that is sent. If they cannot agree, they must suffer a penalty for bothering their bosses, and the issue then goes to their bosses (the two Secretaries) who can send any cable they can agree upon. But if they cannot reach an agreement either, they each suffer a penalty for bothering the President, and he makes a unilateral decision. In general, each of the five people involved in this process may have different views on which cable should be sent and may make different judgments on the relative desirability of the possible compromises that may be proposed. Also, the penalty for having to bother one's boss may be different for each of the four people who have bosses.

Both of the subordinates would like to be able to reach an agreement to avoid having to bother their bosses and to be sure that the decision reflects *their* policy preferences. Their difficulty, however, is that typically their policy preferences are not identical. Similarly their bosses want to settle the issue at their level if it comes to them, but their views of what is the best decision also may differ.

Not surprisingly, the formalization of conflict of interest that has been developed in the theoretical part of this study can now be employed to analyze just how difficult a time the subordinates can be expected to have in reaching an agreement. Likewise, it can be used to analyze the bargaining process between the Secretaries should the issue come to them.

SPECIFICATION OF THE MODEL

The specification of the model in game theoretic terms is required before the formalization of conflict of interest can be extended to cover the bureaucratic policy process. To make this specification manageable, it will be assumed that the officials at the lower level are able to guess at the policy outcome if they themselves are unable to agree and have to refer the issue to their superiors. The guess need not be

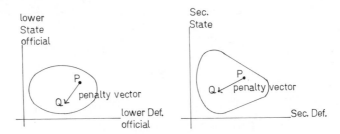

FIGURE 6-2. Two Bargaining Stages
(unnormalized)

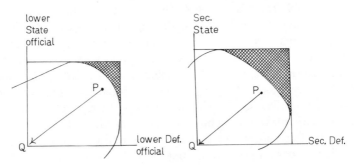

FIGURE 6-3. Two Bargaining Stages
(normalized)

correct, but it must be shared by the other official at the same level.[1]
Then if no agreement is reached, the lower officials know what to
expect in the way of policy as well as how much they will suffer for
bothering their bosses.   This means that as far as the subordinates
are concerned, a single predetermined outcome will result if they cannot
reach an agreement.   This of course, is the very definition of a bargaining game, since it is also natural to assume that the lower officials
can talk to each other and make binding agreements by just signing
their names to a draft of the cable.   If the lower level officials cannot
reach an agreement, the issue comes to the Secretaries.   When this
happens the Secretaries are assumed to be able to guess what the President will decide if they cannot agree,[2] and hence they too would play

---

[1] A weaker assumption, which is also sufficient for the present purposes,
is that the subordinates are able to guess only a probability distribution over the
range of possible outcomes.   For each official, the expected utility of this distribution serves as a "certainty equivalent" to a point estimate of what his boss
will do with the issue.

[2] Again, a probability distribution will suffice, and the guess need not be
right, only shared.   Chapter 4 and the appendix to Chapter 5 offer suggestions
on how expectations and utilities might be measured.

a bargaining game. In this simple model, the President decides the issue for himself if his subordinates cannot agree, although Neustadt (1960) points out that in practice even the President does not have such complete control over all of his subordinates.

The two bargaining games are illustrated in Figure 6-2, and are repeated in normalized form in Figure 6-3. The null point (Q) in each game is derived by subtracting the penalties from the point representing the expected policy outcome if no agreement is reached at that level (P). The penalty vector (or arrow) in the figures is simply a graphical representation of the idea that each side will suffer a penalty for bothering their respective bosses if they (the subordinates) cannot reach an agreement between themselves.

The analysis of conflict of interest in the two bargaining stages of the model of the bureaucratic policy process requires nothing new because this part of the model is merely two bargaining games in sequence with the second to be played only if no agreement is reached in the first. The conflict of interest between the two lower officials (i.e., between the two departments at the lower level) can be determined by the area beyond the region of feasible agreements in the normalized version of the game (the shaded area in the left-hand section of Figure 6-3). The same can be done to measure the conflict of interest between the departments at the level of the Secretaries (the shaded area in the right half of Figure 6-3). While a variety of specific hypothesis might be formulated for the likelihood of different types of conflictful behavior, the most straightforward one is that the more conflict of interest there is at a given level, the more likely the issue will not be settled at that level if it comes there, and instead will have to be referred upward for a decision.

FURTHER APPLICATIONS

Although the simple model that has been discussed so far was derived from the cable clearing process, it applies to a wide variety of bureaucratic policy formation processes. For example, the construction of the annual budget typically follows a similar pattern. Officials within any given department try to reach an agreement with their corresponding officials in the Bureau of the Budget on what the next year's proposed budget for that department should be. If no agreement can be reached at that level, the issue has to be referred to a higher level, such as the head of the department and the Director of the Bureau of the Budget. If they cannot agree the President must decide. As in the cable-clearing process, an agreement at any given level will generally be acceptable to the higher levels.   Indeed, the model applies to almost any area in which an agreement reached by subordinates will be accepted by their bosses and in which the bosses must consider the issue if their subordinates do not reach an agreement.

C. The Prebargaining Stages

SETTING PENALTIES FOR FAILURE

When the lower officials play their bargaining game, there is a fixed penalty for each if they are unable to reach an agreement and have to bother their bosses with the issue.   So far these penalties have been taken as given, but it seems reasonable to suppose that each official's penalty can in fact be controlled by his boss.   A useful assumption is that the bosses set these penalties before the subordinates consider the issue.   This assumption helps keep the model manageable, but prevents it from dealing with the fact that the actual penalties for failure may also be affected by what the subordinates themselves do with the issue and by influences outside the bureaucracy.   Despite these possible effects, a boss usually maintains primary control over the penalty his subordinate suffers for failure to resolve an issue at his own level.

The boss's control over his subordinate's penalty raises the question of how the boss should use this control.   If he sets a large penalty, his subordinate will be very anxious to reach an agreement.   This has the benefit of saving the boss's valuable time.

Other considerations may enter into the boss's utility for having to consider an issue at his level.   He may, for example, actually want to consider an issue to gain information on the subject.   In any case, the strategic structure of the interaction remains unchanged as long as there is some agreement the lower officials can reach which the boss prefers to considering the issue himself.

Likewise, considerations other than strategic ones may enter into the setting of penalties.   For example, the boss may be reluctant to set a high penalty for fear of harming his relations with his subordinate. However, this too could be taken into account in the measurement of his utility function and would not necessarily alter the structure of the strategic relationships.

The boss presumably wants his subordinate to be in a strong bargaining position because his subordinate's policy preferences are usually much closer to his own than are the policy preferences of the other boss's subordinate.   Thus while a large penalty for his subordinate is advantageous to the boss in that it conserves his valuable time, it is disadvantageous in that the subordinate may compromise away many of the policy differences between the two agencies in his desire to reach an agreement. Conversely, a low penalty for failure will let the subordinate be a tough bargainer, but it will also increase the probability that the boss himself will have to spend time on the issue.

Of course, the other boss has a penalty to set as well. If both penalties are set high, there is an excellent chance the subordinates will reach an agreement. This is so because the larger the penalty is, the lower the null point in the subordinates' bargaining game. The lower the null point, the less conflict of interest there tends to be, as was shown in Chapter 2.[3] Also, when both penalties are large neither side can expect a lopsided compromise. If both penalties are small there is a greater chance that no agreement will be reached, but again neither side can expect a lopsided agreement in its favor. So two high penalties are better for both bosses than two low penalties because of the greater chance of agreement among the subordinates. However, if one penalty is set low while the other is high, the subordinate with the low penalty is likely to win a lopsided agreement because the other subordinate is under heavy pressure to compromise.[4] This looks very much as if the upper-level officials are in a Prisoner's Dilemma game, and indeed under certain conditions that is exactly what the relationship between the bosses is when they come to set their subordinates' penalties.

THE PRISONER'S DILEMMA BETWEEN BOSSES

Several requirements must be fulfilled in order for the strategic interaction of setting the penalties to be a Prisoner's Dilemma. The first requirement for a Prisoner's Dilemma is that the players have no way of making binding agreements. This seems to be a realistic assumption in the present case because even if the bosses agree to cooperate by setting high penalties for their subordinates, neither can be sure that the other will not later lower his subordinate's penalty in order to gain a bargaining advantage for him.

The other requirements for a Prisoner's Dilemma refer to the

---

[3] This tendency disappears only if there are complete side payments or their equivalent because then the conflict of interest is at its maximum in the bargaining game no matter where the no agreement point is.

[4] This proposition can be deduced from any one of a number of solution concepts, such as the Nash point. However, for present purposes a formal deduction is not necessary.

parameters involved, and they are (from Chapter 3):

$$T > R > P > S, \quad \text{and}$$
$$2R > S + T$$

(Definition of Prisoner's Dilemma).

The value of each of these parameters depends on two things. One is the utilities to the bosses of the different possible settlements their subordinates can reach. The other is the relative likelihood of these different settlements and of no settlement by the subordinates in each of the four possible bargaining games the subordinates can be made to play. Figure 6-4 shows these four bargaining games between the

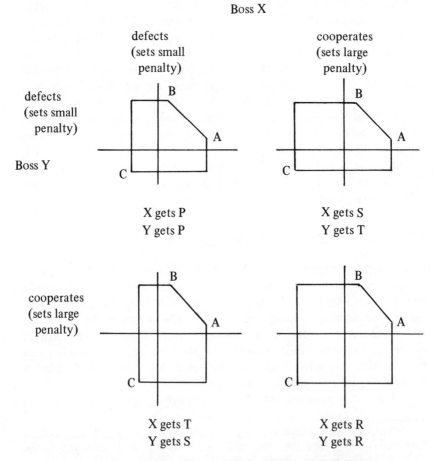

FIGURE 6-4. Bosses X and Y Play Prisoner's Dilemma to Determine Which Bargaining Game Will Be Played by Their Subordinates

subordinates within the matrix of the bosses' game over which penalties are to be set. Boss X sets the penalty for his subordinate, and boss Y sets the penalty for his subordinate. The outcome of this game is the determination of which bargaining game the subordinates play.

To keep the analysis as simple as possible, the policy issue represented in the figure has only two elementary feasible settlements. These agreements are labeled A and B. Outcome A is preferred by Boss X and his subordinate while B is preferred by Y and his subordinate.

In each bargaining game there are three possible outcomes including the null point (labeled C in Figure 6-4). A boss's payoff in a particular game is the sum of the products of the likelihood of each of these outcomes times the utility to him of the corresponding outcome. (This is a consequence of the way utility was defined in Chapter 1.) For instance, if X defects and Y cooperates, X gets T which is

$$T = P_{TA}U_A + P_{TB}U_B + P_{TC}U_C,$$

where P_{TA} is the probability of A being the outcome of the corresponding bargaining game (i.e., the game in the lower left in Figure 6-4) and U_A is the utility to X of outcome A. Without loss of generality the zero and unit points of X's utility schedule can be chosen (see Chapter 1), so for convenience let the zero be the least preferred outcome, i.e., $U_C = 0$, and the unit be the most preferred, i.e., $U_A = 1$. Then using these values,

$$T = P_{TA} + P_{TB}U_B.$$

Likewise, X's payoffs from the other bargaining games are in order of decreasing utility:

$$R = P_{RA} + P_{RB}U_B,$$
$$P = P_{PA} + P_{PB}U_B,$$
$$S = P_{SA} + P_{SB}U_B.$$

If the bosses' game of setting penalties is a Prisoner's Dilemma these parameters must satisfy the inequalities stated earlier defining the Prisoner's Dilemma.

There are two other conditions that have already been discussed and can now be formalized. The first is that X's subordinate is more likely to win his preferred policy outcome, A, if he has a small penalty while Y's subordinate is burdened with a high penalty, rather than vice versa.   Symbolically this can be stated simply as:

$$P_{TA} > P_{SA}.$$

The other condition is just an application of the general hypothesis for bargaining games, namely that other things being equal the more conflict of interest there is, the more likely no agreement will be reached.   Conflict of interest is highest when both penalties are small (when X gets P) and lowest when both are large (when X gets R). This gives:

$$P_{PC} > P_{SC} = P_{TC} > P_{RC}.$$

These last two conditions can also be regarded as two expectations the bosses have about their subordinates.   The first is that if the two subordinates have unequal penalties for failure, the one with the smaller penalty is in a stronger bargaining position.   The second expectation is that the subordinates are least likely to settle the dispute at their own level if they both have small penalties, and most likely to if both have big penalties.

D. Dynamics of the Model

THE FIVE STAGES

The dynamics of the multilevel policy formation model are interesting.   The actual bargaining over the policy outcome begins at the lower level, and if no agreement is reached there it is referred to the upper level.   If the upper level cannot agree, the President decides.   Thus, policy is considered at progressively higher levels.   However, before the bargaining games are played, the penalties for bothering one's boss are set for each subordinate.   The President unilaterally sets the penalties for the upper level officials who are his subordinates, and then they set the penalties for the lower level officials who are their subordinates. Thus the full sequence is:

1. President unilaterally sets upper-level officials' penalties,
2. Upper-level officials set lower-level officials' penalties (in what may be a Prisoner's Dilemma game),
3. Lower-level officials play bargaining game to determine the policy outcome,
4. Upper-level officials play bargaining game to determine the policy outcome if the lower-level officials were unable to agree,

5. President unilaterally decides the issue if the upper-level officials are unable to agree.

CONFLICT OF INTEREST WITHIN EACH STAGE

The first and last stages involve only one person, the President, so they are not games at all and have no conflict of interest.[5]   However, each of the other stages is a strategic interaction with a conflict of interest that is not difficult to calculate with the definitions developed in Part I of this study.   The amount of conflict of interest can be used to predict certain aspects of behavior at these stages, and the elements of the calculation of conflict of interest can be used to reveal certain properties of these interactions.

After the President sets the penalties for the upper-level officials in the first stage, the second stage consists of the upper-level officials setting the penalties for the lower-level officials.   If the game between the bosses fulfills the conditions of a Prisoner's Dilemma, then in the second stage

$$\text{conflict of interest} = \frac{(T - R)(T - S)}{(T - P)^2}$$ (Prisoner's Dilemma between bosses over setting penalties).

As mentioned earlier, the four parameters of this formula can be calculated in terms of the bosses' utilities for the final policy outcomes and their expectations concerning the likelihood of their subordinates' arriving at each of these possible agreements.

Even without tracing this formula for conflict of interest at the second stage back to its fundamental elements, one can see several of its implications.   For example, the larger the factor $T - R$ is, the more conflict of interest there is.   The factor $T - R$ is just the gain to a boss for double-crossing the other boss, i.e., the gain for setting a low rather than a high penalty while the other boss cooperates by giving his subordinate a high penalty.   Using the general hypothesis for the Prisoner's Dilemma, one concludes that the greater the incentive for one boss to double cross the other is, the more likely low penalties will be set.   To go one step further, the general hypothesis could then

---

[5] Incidentally, if the entire five stage process is regarded as a single game, the conflict of interest at each stage should properly be called the "restricted conflict of interest" that is relevant to that stage. Alternatively, the whole process can be regarded as a sequence of related but separate, games, making the conflict of interest at each stage total rather than restricted.   The choice is arbitrary, so for convenience the second point of view is taken.

be applied to the next stage, the bargaining game between the subordinates. At that stage low penalties mean high conflict of interest and thus high probability of failure. Putting these results together yields the conclusion that the greater the gain is for one boss to double-cross the other in the setting of penalties for subordinates at the second stage, the more likely that later the bosses themselves will have to bargain over the substance of the issue.

The conflict of interest between the subordinates when they bargain in stage three depends upon two considerations: their relative preferences for the different feasible policy outcomes and the size of their penalties for failure to reach an agreement. The subordinates play one of the four bargaining games displayed in Figure 6-4. Which one they play depends on which penalties are set. For example, Figure 6-5 repeats the case shown in the lower left of Figure 6-4. This is the situation in which boss X has set a small penalty for his subordinate and boss Y has set a big penalty for his. The conflict of interest in this bargaining game is readily measured by the ratio of the infeasible triangle (shaded in Figure 6-5) to the area of the large rectangle.

Again, without even performing the actual calculations, one can easily derive a number of results. For example, in all four cases the smaller the infeasible area, the less conflict of interest there is between the subordinates. Thus the more X's subordinate likes the most preferred policy of Y's subordinate (i.e., the further point B is to the right), the less conflict of interest there is. Likewise the better Y's subordinate thinks of outcome A, the less conflict of interest there is. Of course, according to the general hypothesis for bargaining games, the less conflict of interest there is between the subordinates, the more likely they can settle the issue between themselves.

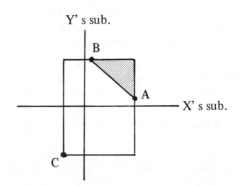

FIGURE 6-5. X Has Set a Small Penalty
and Y Has Set a Big Penalty

If, however, the subordinates fail to reach an agreement their bosses have to consider the substance of the issue in stage four. The bosses' consideration of the issue takes place in the context of a bargaining game between them. The conflict of interest at this stage depends on the bosses' policy preferences and the penalties the President has set for them. Since this is another bargaining game the conflict of interest can readily be measured, and the factors influencing the amount of conflict of interest can readily be analyzed (see Figure 6-6).

E. Embellishments of the Basic Model

The basic model can be embellished in a number of ways to make it a better approximation of a wider variety of bureaucratic bargaining processes.

ADDITIONAL LEVELS OF OFFICIALS

The simplest addition is to allow more than two layers of bureaucracy below the President. Figure 6-7 schematically shows the State and Defense Departments with four levels each. As before, the corresponding model is a sequence of games to set penalties starting at the top and working down, followed by a sequence of bargaining games starting at the bottom and working up. The only difference is that now these sequences are longer and so there are more stages in the model.

ADDITIONAL AGENCIES

Frequently more than two agencies are involved in a given decision and agreement among all of them is necessary for action. (See

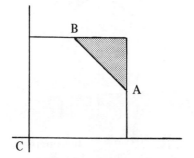

FIGURE 6-6. Bosses' Bargaining
Game (Stage 4)

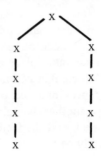

FIGURE 6-7. Bureaucracy
with Four Levels
below the President

Figure 6-8.) The only change that needs to be made in the model is to indicate that each of the games (whether for setting penalties or bargaining over policy) has more than two players. This causes no difficulty in the analysis because methods of calculating conflict of interest in n-person Prisoner's Dilemmas and bargaining games have already been developed (see p. 72). Thus, a bureaucracy arbitrarily "deep" and arbitrarily "wide" can be readily treated by easy extensions of the basic model, by adding more stages to the model and letting each of the game stages include more players.

PYRAMIDAL HIERARCHY

Often more than one part of a department is involved in an issue that also involves other departments. Then the schematic view of the people who have a say in the policy process is no longer a set of

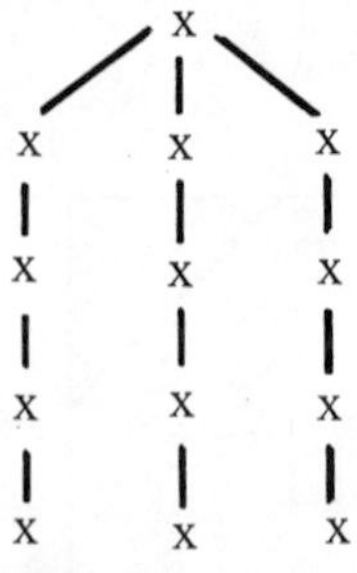

FIGURE 6-8. Bureaucracy
with Three Agencies
Each with Four Levels

parallel chains under the President, but is instead a tree or pyramid, as shown in Figure 6-9.

In this case, either of two procedures might be employed to determine the roles of the various officials. The first is that a decision simply requires acceptance by all the people at any level; otherwise the decision is referred to the next level. The appropriate model is then a sequence of bargaining games, but with fewer and fewer players participating in each one. In the situation portrayed in Figure 6-9, for example, the lowest level consists of a six-person bargaining game, the next has three persons, and the next two.

The other procedure would be used if a boss insists that all his subordinates must reach an agreement on a common position before bargaining with anyone from another part of the bureaucracy. If they cannot reach such an agreement the boss would have to determine one for himself before bargaining with others (and the subordinates would suffer the penalty for causing him the extra bother). To return to Figure 6-9 again, x_7, x_8, and x_9 would first bargain among themselves, as would x_{10} and x_{11}. Then x_5 would use his subordinates' agreement and bargain with x_6. The first time the entire decision could be made is when x_2 and x_3 get together.

Of course, these two procedures could be used simultaneously but by different parts of the bureaucracy, with some agencies insisting on unified positions before bargaining with outsiders, and others letting different parts of their agency bargain independently. In any case, the conflict of interest at each bargaining stage can be determined in the usual way because each of these stages is a simple bargaining game. As far as setting penalties is concerned, each boss controls all of his subordinates' penalties and this raises no serious problems in the analysis. So the basic model can easily be extended to treat any kind of pyramidal hierarchy of officials involved in an issue as well as the simple situation of parallel chains of officials treated originally.

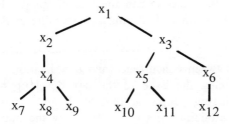

FIGURE 6-9. A Pyramidal Bureaucracy

CONCURRENCE AND COORDINATION

In bureaucratic terminology concurrence means veto power (i.e., power to force an issue to the next level up), but coordination means only the right to be consulted before a decision is made. For an issue on a given subject, past usage usually allows everyone in the bureaucracy to agree on just who has which right.

So far, the model of bargaining in bureaucracies has dealt only with concurrences. To allow the treatment of coordination as well, one need only assume that an agency with only the power to coordinate cannot force the issue to another level, but that the agency's failure to agree on a solution with another agency will impose an additional penalty on both agencies. For example, a cable on financial arrangements in NATO may require the concurrence of the State Department and the Defense Department but only the coordination of the Treasury Department. State and Defense have an incentive to attain Treasury's approval, but it is not absolutely necessary to get it.

In actual practice, there often is very little distinction between the two powers of concurrence and coordination. Agencies sometimes seem almost as anxious to reach agreement with other agencies that can only coordinate as they are to secure the approval of agencies that have the full veto power of withholding concurrence. And sometimes almost as much will be compromised to attain one as to attain the other.

To understand why this should be so, consider the case of an issue involving only two agencies, one of which can only coordinate. If the main agency fails to get the other's agreement on some compromise, it will certainly make the decision it prefers most of all (point A in Figure 6-10). In that case, both sides would suffer a penalty for not reaching an agreement and the net payoffs would be at point B. So if no agreement is reached both sides know that the result will be B. This means that the coordinating agency can, in effect, veto any agreement other than B. And so can the main agency. In other words, the two agencies are indeed playing a bargaining game with the null point at B.

This explains why agencies can sometimes be unconcerned about the distinction between concurrence and coordination. Both are veto powers: one forcing the issue to the next level up and imposing a penalty for bothering people at that level, and the other forcing a penalty for not attaining approval. Typically the null point is lower for an official when he has to get someone else's concurrence. Then there is not only a direct penalty to pay, but this penalty is subtracted

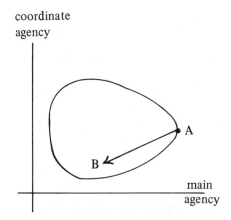

FIGURE 6-10.   Coordination Game

from a point that may be substantially less desirable than that official's optimal policy choice.   So an official typically prefers that the others who are involved at his level have only the power to coordinate and not concur.   However, if the penalty for not getting agreement from an agency with the power to concur is great enough, the distinction is relatively unimportant.

F. Long Run Considerations

OPERATING STYLES

One of the most important features of the policy formation process in bureaucracies is that everyone knows the bureaucracy is almost certain to be in existence tomorrow, next month, and next year.   This means that every issue is treated as only one among many issues, rather than as an isolated problem.   The basic model and the embellishments on it are essentially tools for analyzing one issue at a time.   However, the model is also capable of dealing with long-range considerations by analyzing factors that may be common to many different issues.

For example, officials may have very stable operating styles that help determine how they approach the question of setting penalties for their subordinates.   A comparison of Roosevelt and Eisenhower is illustrative of this point (Neustadt, 1960, 156–161).   Roosevelt's style was to keep jurisdictional boundaries uncertain and to put men of differing outlooks in charge of the overlapping jurisdictions "making his subordinates push up to him the choices they could not take for themselves."   Eisenhower preferred "men who told each other (and themselves), 'don't bother the boss,' 'can't do this to him now'." Roosevelt's style gave him the ability to make key choices himself. In contrast, Eisenhower's style was to set very high penalties.

> Eisenhower, seemingly, preferred to let subordinates proceed upon the lowest common denominators of agreement than to have their quarrels—and issues and details—pushed up to him. (Neustadt, 1960, 161)

PATTERNED PREFERENCES

Another factor that may be constant over a large number of issues is the policy preferences of the officials. These individual preferences are likely to be closely related to the official's place in the bureaucracy, according to the old saw that "where you stand depends upon where you sit." For example, officials in the State Department may give special weight to maintaining good relations with allies, while officials in the Defense Department might give more weight to the adequacy of our military posture. Conceivably such differences in emphasis could be used to help specify utility schedules of the participants for many issues at once. Possibly agencies (or at least levels of agencies) could be placed in a policy space with dimensions different in substantive content, but in structure much like the liberal-conservative dimension so frequently used to discuss Congressional and popular policy preferences. Even if such a space required two or three dimensions it would be a great aid in relating specific issues to one another.

SCARCE TIME

One of the most important relationships between different issues is that they all compete for an official's scarce time. The higher up an official is in a bureaucracy, the broader his area of involvement is and hence the more issues come within his domain. If an official's subordinates (and perhaps his subordinates' subordinates) brought every issue they dealt with to him he would be utterly swamped. So to preserve his time, the official must encourage his subordinates to dispose of as many issues as possible at their own level. This need to avoid considering each and every issue is what lies behind the notion of a boss imposing a penalty upon a subordinate whenever he cannot dispose of the issue at his own level. Thus the competition between issues for the official's scarce time is already built into the basic model.

HIERARCHICAL CONTROL

Of course few bosses want to avoid all issues. The more typical case is illustrated by the bugetary process. A boss does not want to handle too many budgetary issues, but he does want to handle some of them. If too many issues move up to his level, the boss can increase the penalties for no agreement to discourage his subordinate from continually flooding him with issues. However, if his subordinate is doing a good job of resolving issues at the lower level, the boss can set lower penalties on subsequent issues so that at least a few issues will move up to his level. Thus a boss can raise or lower the penalties he sets in order to decrease or increase the number of issues he will have to consider personally.

POWER RELATIONSHIPS

Another long run consideration that can be treated (at least in part) with the basic model is that of the power relationships among the various agencies. In particular, the model suggests that three factors that tend to make an official in an agency weak in his bargaining relationships are:

1. An unusually high penalty for bothering his boss,
2. A boss with substantially different policy preferences, and
3. A boss who is weak himself in either of these two respects.

SALUTARY BELIEFS

Finally, there are a number of stable factors that tend to lower the relative or absolute amount of conflict of interest in bargaining over policy which have not yet been mentioned. First, officials who lose on a particular usually issue are gracious in their defeat, so most issues are not compounded by recriminations or ill feeling. This graciousness is promoted by the knowledge that usually everyone gets at least a fair hearing, and that the same people will have to deal with each other again many times in the future. Second, the magnitude of the stakes on any given issue is reduced by the fact that most issues of any significance are likely to arise again in the future. Thus the whole issue is not settled once and for all by any one bargaining outcome. Third, officials are typically quite uncertain about what a particular governmental policy will actually bring when implemented. One effect of this uncertainty is that no official can be sure his preferred policy would really be the best one, even from his own point of view, and thus the stakes are again reduced. Another effect of uncertainty about the results of a decision is that officials are open to persuasion by other officials. Finally, conflict of interest between officials in different agencies is reduced by the widespread belief among bureaucrats that there is indeed something which can be called the "public interest" or the "national interest." This outlook leads to the feeling that if one agency loses badly on an issue the whole government loses. Such a feeling naturally tends to reduce the conflict of interest between different agencies. These four factors which tend to reduce the relative or absolute conflict of interest between officials supplement the earlier point that high penalties for bothering one's boss also tend to lower (relative) conflict of interest. Against all these factors must be placed the fact that different agencies usually have somewhat different policy preferences, so some conflict of interest is bound to exist on most issues.

G. Summary

Bureaucracies are not monolithic organizations rationally pursuing a single goal. Instead, they decompose problems and assign different subproblems to different parts of the organization. The decomposition can rarely be perfect; interactions between the subproblems nearly always remain. To achieve some degree of coordination between the subproblems, the different parts of a bureaucracy involved in the problem bargain with each other, usually with biases associated with their location in the organization. If the subordinates cannot reach an agreement, their bosses must consider the issue.

Using the building blocks of the bargaining game and the Prisoner's Dilemma game, a basic model has been constructed to describe this process of multilevel decisionmaking. Since these are the two kinds of games for which conflict of interest has been defined in Part I, the multiple stages of the model could be analyzed in terms of conflict of interest.

Next, the basic model was extended so that it could treat structures of officials involved in a given issue that were arbitrarily deep and wide, and even pyramidal. Then treatment of officials with only the right to be consulted (coordination) was added to the treatment of officials with a full veto power (concurrence).

Finally, some long run considerations that affect many different issues were discussed. These long run considerations include the operating styles of the bosses in setting penalties for their subordinates, the stable patterns of policy preferences of officials in the bureaucracy, the impact of the scarcity of time, the adjustment of penalties to control the flow of issues, power relationships between parts of the bureaucracy, and a number of common salutary beliefs that tend to lower absolute or relative conflict of interest of bargaining in bureaucracies.

7

Spatial Models
of Society

A. Conflict of Interest in Society

AN EXAMPLE OF THE ANALYTIC PROBLEM

One of the fundamental themes in Western political thought is the relationship between the common interests and the divergent interests of the members of a political community. Concepts resembling conflict of interest often play an important part in the analytic treatments of this theme.

As an example, take the issue of how large a democracy should be. A number of classical and modern authors treat this question in terms closely related to conflict of interest. Aristotle argued that too large a polity could not remain orderly:

> Law is a system of order; and a general habit of obedience to law must therefore involve a general system of orderliness. Order, however, is the one thing which is impossible for an excessive number. (trans. Barker, 1962, 291)

One of Rousseau's arguments for a small civil state in his *Social Contract* relies directly on the idea of conflict of interest:

> The same laws cannot suit so many diverse provinces with different customs, situated in the most various climates, and incapable of enduring a uniform government.   (trans. Cole, 1950, 45)

In arguing for a large representative republic, Madison also gives an analysis in terms of common and divergent interests.   The argument is clearest in *Federalist* No. 10:

> The smaller the society, the fewer probably will be the distinct parties and interests composing it; the fewer the distinct parties and interests, the more frequently will a majority be found of the same party; and the smaller the number of individuals composing a majority, and the smaller the compass within which they are placed, the more easily will they concert and execute their plans of oppression.   Extend the sphere and you take in a greater variety of parties and interests; you make it less probable that a majority of the whole will have a common motive to invade the rights of other citizens. . . .   (Madison, 1787)

A modern democractic theorist, Dahl, also deals with the question of the ideal size of a democracy in terms similar to conflict of interest. He suggests that

> the most rational rule to follow would appear to be something like this: Select a political society that contains individuals whose goals are sufficiently like your own to provide the highest probability that you will maximize all your key values.   (1956, 53–54)

Other issues in addition to those relating to conflict of interest are also important to these and other authors in the determination of the optimum size of a democracy.   Among these other issues are economic and military viability, and the coordination problems associated with size.   Although issues relating to conflict of interest are not the sole criteria for the normative judgments of these authors, they are certainly among the central considerations.

In their analysis of political communities, these and many other authors have used concepts related to conflict of interest.   However, as the review of the literature on this subject in Chapter 1 has shown, no one has provided a formalization of the meaning of conflict of interest which can be used to treat these questions in the context of modern models of strategic interaction.   The goal of this chapter is to provide such a formalization for conflict of interest at the societal level by extending the earlier definition of conflict of interest, and then applying this formal concept to several important topics in democratic theory.

Another example of why this formalization might be useful is suggested by Dahrendorf (1959).   He identified two (meta-) theories of society: the integration theory and the coercion theory.

> The notions of interest and value indeed seem to describe very well the two faces of the normative superstructure of society: what appears as a consensus of values on the basis of the integration theory can be regarded as a conflict of interests in terms of the coercion theory.   (163)

> Inevitably, the question will be raised, also, whether a unified theory of society that includes the tenets of both the integration and coercion models of society is not at least conceivable— for as to its desirability there can be little doubt.   (164)

Since the integration and coercion theories stress respectively low and high amounts of conflict of interest in society, perhaps the quantification of conflict of interest can be used in a future effort to synthesize these theories.

OUTLINE OF THE CHAPTER

The extension to the societal level of the definition of conflict of interest will be done in the context of a spatial model of society. First the model will be specified and then the familiar notion of conflict of interest in a two-person bargaining game will be related to this model.   The meaning of conflict of interest for an entire society can then be readily described.   The result is quite simple and provides a convenient way of comparing alternative distributions of public policy preferences.

Two specific applications of the formal concept will be treated in detail.   The first is the question of how apportionment should be performed in representative democracies, and the second is a treatment of the theory of crosscutting and overlapping cleavages.

B. Formalization of the Concept

SPATIAL MODELS OF SOCIETY

In 1789, when the French National Assembly convened, the nobles still retained sufficient respect to be given places of honor to the right of the president. The radicals took seats in the amphitheater as far away from the nobles as they could, placing themselves on the left. The moderates found themselves occupying the remaining seats in the center. Thus began the now familiar political dimension of left–center–right.

This dimension, or any other policy dimension for that matter (such as pro- and anti-clerical, or isolationist–internationalist), can be conveniently treated in terms of a spatial model. The advantage of such a treatment is that a great deal can be said about politics in the relatively easy terminology of positions on and movements along such a dimension.

The first extended formal treatment of such a spatial model in politics was developed by Downs (1957, 115ff.), who borrowed and elaborated upon an apparatus invented by the economist Hotelling (1929). In Downs' version of the model, there is a political dimension running on a cardinal scale from zero to 100. He assumes that political positions can be ordered from left to right by all voters in the same way, although they need not agree on which point they personally prefer. His third assumption is that between two points on the same side of his optimum position, a voter prefers the point which is closer to his optimum point.

For the purposes of this chapter, two changes will be made in Downs' model, one a generalization and one a restriction. The generalization is suggested by Sartori (1966, 138), who notes that in some societies the distance between the extremities of a political dimension may be greater than in other societies. The assumption of a scale from zero to 100 is therefore misleading, and should be dropped. The restriction is the tightening of Downs' assumption about distance. It shall be assumed that the utility loss caused by moving away from one's optimum position not only increases, but increases linearly with distance along the scale. While this assumption is unlikely to be completely accurate, it does make the application of conflict of interest to the spatial model of society easier than it would otherwise be.

Criticisms of spatial models have been made. In what is perhaps the most thorough and most sophisticated critique of the Hotelling–Downs model, Srokes follows his specific objections with this statement:

> The conclusion I would draw from all this is not that the spatial model should be rejected root-and-branch but rather that we should treat as explicit variables the cognitive phenomena that the prevailing model removes from the discussion by assumption. (1963, 376)

Treating cognitive phenomena explicitly would certainly improve the spatial model, but for now even the basic spatial model is useful for analyzing conflict of interest in society.   The same criticism and the same reply could be made for the analysis of conflict of interest as it is treated in the present study: it would be better if cognitive phenomena (such as how people come to see what their preferences are) were treated explicitly, but even the basic version of the theory is useful in the analysis of a variety of political processes.

CONFLICT OF INTEREST BETWEEN TWO PEOPLE

The task at hand is to extend the definition of conflict of interest to cover conflict of interest at the societal level.   In order to do this, the spatial model of society was introduced.   Now the familiar meaning of conflict of interest between two people in a bargaining game will be related to this spatial model, and then this result will be generalized to apply to very large numbers of people.

Suppose two people, x and y, are in a bargaining game situation over what policy position along a given dimension should be adopted. Figure 7-1 shows such a dimension with five equally spaced points marked with the letters A through E.   Suppose x's most preferred policy position is at C and y's best point is at B.   Then the corresponding normalized bargaining game would look like the one on the left in Figure 7-2.

Now suppose y stays at B but x's most preferred point moves from C to D.   The new positions and the corresponding bargaining game are shown on the right half of Figure 7-2.   Note that in the representation of the bargaining game, the y coordinate of each alternative is unchanged because y's best alternative is unchanged.   The x coordinates are changed to reflect the movement of x's best position from C to D.   Note also that this movement causes both the width and the height of the conflict of interest triangle to double, thus causing its area to quadruple.   (It is assumed here that x and y each prefer the other's best outcome to no agreement.)   Thus a doubling of the distance between the two people's preferred policy positions yields a quadrupling of the conflict of interest.   Or to put it formally, the following theorem has just been demonstrated:

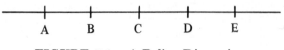

FIGURE 7-1.   A Policy Dimension

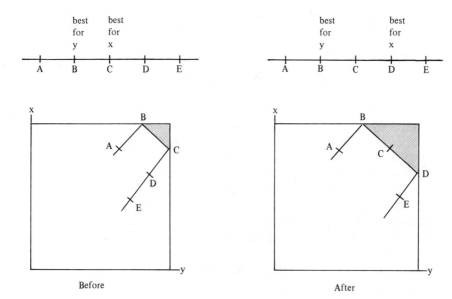

FIGURE 7-2. How Conflict of Interest Changes
If X's Preference Moves From C to D

Theorem. Assuming a spatial model where each person's utility loss is proportional to the distance from his optimum position, and assuming that each person prefers the other's best outcome to no agreement, then conflict of interest in a two-person bargaining game is proportional to the square of the distance between the two people.

CONFLICT OF INTEREST FOR LARGE NUMBERS

The spatial model of society views the members of the society as a distribution of people along a policy dimension, with each person placed at the position he most prefers. An illustration is given in Figure 7-3. It has just been shown how the conflict of interest between

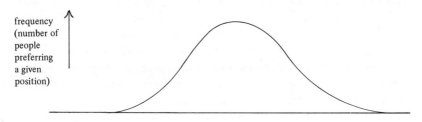

FIGURE 7-3. Preferred Positions of People
in a Society

two of these people can be defined. These two people can be used to represent any pair of people in the society. Now conflict of interest in the entire society can be defined.

Definition. Conflict of interest in society on a given policy dimension is the average conflict of interest between a pair of people, as each one of the pair takes on all the positions in the policy dimension in proportion to the position's frequency in the society.

This formulation goes beyond the game theory context that has been employed so far in this study. Although this interpretation of conflict of interest in society does depend upon the preferences of the participants, it does not mention the strategies available to the members of society to achieve their goals, nor does it specify the nature of the strategic interaction within the society. It does not assume, for example, that the members of society are in one huge bargaining game in which every individual has veto power. The approach used merely suggests that a fruitful way to think about topics such as consensus and cleavage in a society is in terms of the conflict of interest in that society.

Using an average implies reliance on the same assumptions just made for the two-person case, including the assumption that every person prefers anyone else's optimum position to no agreement at all. In the case of a whole society, this can be interpreted as an assumption of pragmatic politics rather than revolutionary or anti-system behavior. Because of this assumption, the particular way in which conflict of interest is extended in this chapter to the societal level is not useful in the study of politics in a society in which a significant proportion of the population prefers destruction of the political system to bargaining and compromise.

The definition of conflict of interest in a society is the average conflict of interest between two people in a bargaining game as each takes on all the positions in the policy space in proportion to the positions' frequency in the society. Intuitively, this means that the more spread out or dispersed is the distribution of people along the policy dimension, the more often is the pair far apart. The more often the pair is far apart, the higher is the average conflict of interest between them, and the higher is the conflict of interest for the whole society.

The standard way to measure the amount of dispersion in a distribution is with the statistical definition of variance (*viz.,* the mean squared deviation from the mean). This suggests the question: what is the relationship between conflict of interest in the spatial model of society and the variance of the distribution of people in that model? The answer is given in the following theorem.

Theorem. Conflict of interest in society measures exactly the same thing as does the variance of the distribution.[1] Hence the concepts may be used interchangeably.

The result that conflict of interest in society is the same as variance of the distribution along a policy dimension automatically dispenses with two potential problems: interpersonal comparison of utilities and the meaning of the null point. There is no need for interpersonal comparisons of utility of the different members of society because the only comparisons needed are between the locations of the preferred policy positions of the members of the society.[2] The specific way in which conflict of interest in society has been defined does not depend on the null point except for the assumption that the society must not be subject to anti-system politics in the sense discussed earlier. This independence means that instead of absolute conflict of interest, the more useful (relative) conflict of interest can be used in the analysis of spatial models of society.

Now that conflict of interest has been defined for the societal level, the analysis of conflict of interest can be applied to whole political communities. The concept of conflict of interest is basically a static

---

[1] The proof is brief. The pair of people take on positions x_i and x_j along the policy dimension. In the two-person bargaining game the conflict of interest between them is proportional to the square of the distance between them, i.e.,

$$c.i. = k(x_i - x_j)^2 \qquad \text{pair.}$$

The conflict of interest in society is the average over the distribution of the conflict of interest of this pair, giving

$$c.i. = k\Sigma_i \Sigma_j (x_i - x_j)^2 / N^2 \qquad \text{society.}$$

Even in societies as small as New Haven or Luxembourg, N can be used to replace $N - 1$, as it has been here. Without loss of generality, the constant of proportionality, k, can be taken to be $\frac{1}{2}$. This gives

$$c.i. = \frac{1}{2N^2} (N\Sigma_i x_i{}^2 - 2\Sigma_j \Sigma_i x_i x_j + N\Sigma_j x_j{}^2)$$

$$= \frac{1}{N^2} (N\Sigma_i x_i{}^2 - (\Sigma_i x_i)^2)$$

$$= \text{Var}(x) \qquad \text{society.} \qquad Q.E.D.$$

[2] To prove that the definition of conflict of interest in society does not depend on an interpersonal comparison of utilities it is sufficient to demonstrate that it is independent of the choice of the zero and unit of the individuals' utility schedules. This independence is equivalent to independence of two other parameters: the amount of utility for one's optimum position and the utility loss per unit policy distance. Since the definition of conflict of interest in society depends only on the number of people with optimums at each position, it is independent of the choice of these two parameters.

one, but it can also be used dynamically to analyze changes over time. For example, if a society becomes more polarized on a major policy issue, people move to the extremes, variance of the distribution increases, and therefore societal conflict of interest rises.   In this manner changes in people's policy preferences can be analyzed with the tools developed in this chapter.

The next two sections deal with specific applications of this theory of societal conflict of interest.   The first treats the issues involved in apportionment of legislative districts and the second discusses the theory of cross-cutting and overlapping cleavages.

C. Apportionment

THE PROBLEM

Nearly twenty-five hundred years ago an experiment was conducted in Athens to promote democratic institutions by the deliberate integration of divergent interests.   The experiment is described by Aristotle in his work on *The Athenian Constitution* (trans. Rackam, 1938, 63–65).   The undertaking proved eminently successful, and has significance for the modern political analyst because the procedure can be generalized for application to contemporary problems.

In the sixth century B.C. Athens was subject to the growth of local factions based in the coastal region, the city, and the interior. Cleisthenes invented a new organization that turned out to be practical in greatly reducing the danger of internal discord caused by the diverging interests of the three regions of the state.   He divided each of the regions into ten *trittyes,* and from them formed ten new tribes, each of which was the union of a *trittis* from each of the regions.   Thus each tribe included the same proportion of citizens from each region. The tribes sent fifty men to the Council of Five Hundred, the supreme administrative authority of the state.   This redistricting procedure effectively eliminated the regionally based factions from politics and thereby helped to integrate the society (Bury, 1913, 211ff.).

Contemporary nations face similar problems, but solutions this drastic may not be tolerable or necessary.   Consider the case of a typical underveloped country, such as Burma, trying to build a democracy (Pye, 1962).   The major dimensions of cleavage are expressible in geographical terms.   The modern segment of the nation is largely confined to portions of the capital city.   Ethnic minorities are to a certain extent concentrated in specific regions, and so are various crops and resources.   If representation in the legislature were based on districts drawn to coincide with these various natural regions, the conflicts of interest inherent in the nation would be fully represented in the national government. If, however, the lines of electoral districts were deliberately drawn to blur these national divisions somewhat, the parliamentary candidates would no longer be able to appeal to a relatively uniform constituency. The result might well be more balanced representatives and a measure of integration in the functioning of the national legislature.

CONFLICT OF INTEREST ANALYSIS

A consideration of the question of apportionment in its abstract form will illustrate many of its important aspects, suggest hypotheses that can be tested, and provide insights into political integration. The simplest case is a square country with a policy dimension that corresponds to the east-west axis of the country. Suppose there are twelve legislative districts laid out in north-south strips, as in Figure 7-4. In this case, each representative is elected from a uniform constituency and the legislature contains representatives from each stratum of the policy dimension. Conflict of interest during the local campaigns is minimal, but conflict of interest in the legislature is great. Compare this situation to the one illustrated in Figure 7-5. Now the districts are east-west strips, and each representative comes from a district that is a miniature version of the nation itself. The likely outcome is that local elections would be fiercely fought because all segments of society would participate in each campaign, while the representatives chosen would fall somewhere near the center of the continuum. Since all the representatives would come from districts with similar distributions of attitudes, they themselves are likely to be similar and the national legislature in turn will not be the scene of severe conflict of interest.

ALLOCATION OF ELECTORAL AND LEGISLATIVE CONFLICT OF INTEREST

This analysis leads to the observation that the conflict of interest within a society at a given instant may be apportioned between the electoral level and the legislative level. In the two cases above, all the conflict of interest was put at one level: the first example with its stratified districts left all the conflict of interest to the legislative arena, while the second case with its identical districts had all of its conflict of interest at the level of the individual district. If, as may well be the situation, each level is able to absorb no more than a certain amount of conflict of interest before the disputes at that level

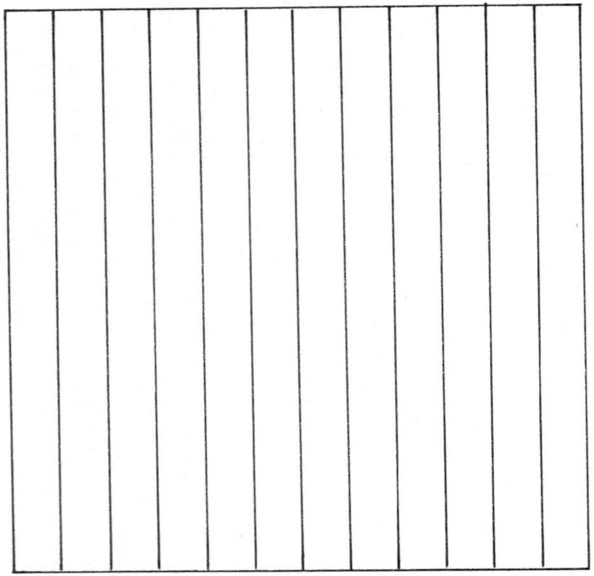

FIGURE 7-5

FIGURE 7-4
Horizontal Axis (East-West) Is Policy Dimension

become too severe for the democratic process to handle, then an appropriate allocation of the conflict of interest between these two levels may help sustain democracy by allowing it to withstand a greater amount of total conflict of interest within the society.

These considerations are often ignored in forming the legislative election districts. The criteria which are typically used are:

1. equal population,
2. compactness,
3. homogeneity, and
4. partisan advantage.

In the United States, for example, the last criterion has frequently been achieved at the expense of the first (through unequal representation) or the second (through gerrymandering). Political scientists tend to regard equal population and compactness as positive values, partisan advantage as negative, and homogeneity as irrelevant. The analysis of conflict of interest given above, however, suggests that homogeneity of electoral districts may have important positive or negative results depending on how the policy preferences within the society are geographically distributed.

Some important factors relevant to policy are geographically distributed in the United States, especially urban-rural and Negro-white. To a lesser but still significant extent the same is true of rich-poor, and liberal-conservative. When non-partisan boundaries are drawn for state legislatures, such as those constructed under court supervision, equal population and compactness are the criteria which are usually maximized. The result may well be that compactness causes homogeneity to be very great and this in turn may cause conflict of interest within the legislature to be greater than is desirable or necessary.

Compactness is accepted as a primary value largely because the blatant employment of partisan advantage in drawing district lines has been associated with districts that are anything but compact. The point of the present analysis is that too much compactness may lead to too much homogeneity. Thus instead of maximizing compactness for its own sake, one should consider the optimum balance between homogeneity and heterogeneity of the districts so that some of the societal conflict of interest will be absorbed by the elections of representatives and some will remain for the legislature to handle. In individual American states, the urban-rural conflict of interest is often severe and the districts for state senator and representative are extremely homogeneous. Thus many elections are almost without conflict of in-

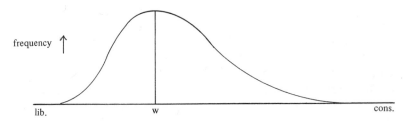

frequency

lib.   w   cons.

FIGURE 7-6.   A Distribution of Preferences on
Liberal-Conservative Policy Dimension

terest on this dimension while the state legislature is the scene of great
conflict of interest over issues that are frequently associated with
urban–rural differences such as taxes, education policy, and welfare
programs.

It should be noted that there may be a lower bound as well as
an upper bound to the amount of conflict of interest that is desirable
at each level.   For example, a moderate amount of conflict of interest
may help clarify the choices a society has in shaping its future.

The next step is to formalize the treatment by providing definitions
for the key terms.   As before, a single dimension of conflict of interest
will be considered.   The procedure works for any policy dimension,
but it should be thought of as applying to one dimension at a time.

Consider people at a certain point of the policy dimension, for
example the people at the modal position on a liberal-conservative
dimension (see Figure 7–6).   If these poeple are in districts composed
entirely of people of very similar liberal-conservative policy position, then there will be little conflict of interest among them on this
issue dimension in the local elections.   However, if these people live
in districts that include many extreme liberals and extreme conservatives,
then the district elections in which they participate will be arenas of
considerable liberal-conservative conflict of interest.

This concept can be formalized as follows: *the conflict of interest
in district elections for people at a given policy position* is a weighted
average conflict of interest in the district, where the weights are proportional to the number of people in each district at that policy position.[3]

---

[3] To put this in algebraic terms, let w be the policy dimension and $Y_i(w)$
be the distribution of voters in the ith district along w. For each of the n districts
the amount of conflict of interest in the district, C_i, is of course the variance of
$Y_i(w)$. The distribution of all voters is $Y(w) = \Sigma_i Y_i(w)$, and the variance
of this is the conflict of interest in society. The conflict of interest in district
elections (for people at w_o) is

$$Z(w_o) = (\Sigma_i Y_i(w_o) \cdot C_i)/Y(w_o).$$

The total conflict of interest in district elections can now be defined as the average conflict of interest in district elections for all people in the society.[4] This also measures the amount of integration done by the district elections. Hence it suggests the definition that the *conflict of interest remaining for the legislature to handle* is the total conflict of interest in society minus the total conflict of interest in district elections.

To estimate the terms used in these definitions, people's complete utility schedules are not required. All that is needed is the number of people in each district who prefer each position on the specific policy dimension. This information can be readily supplied by survey research data, and the computations can be done with the usual statistical procedures for analysis of variance.

This analysis of integration of conflict of interest at the district and national level suggests a number of hypotheses:

1. If the conflict of interest is largely confined to the district level, the issues arising from that policy dimension will not be salient in the national legislature. The reasoning is simply that all representatives will have to appeal to similar constituencies, and hence the legislature will not have members representing grossly different positions along this dimension.

2. If, on the other hand, most of the conflict of interest is at the legislative level, and parties are cohesive and few in number, there will be many one-sided elections. The existence of most of the conflict of interest at the legislative level is equivalent to the homogeneity of each district, that is, each consists of people at a distinct position along the policy dimension. In the extreme districts only one of the national parties will be appealing (assuming cohesiveness of the parties), so the elections there will be one-sided. Conversely, if the elections are tossups in all the districts and there are only a few parties, then high conflict of interest at the legislative level implies that the parties themselves cannot be cohesive nationally.

3. If the district integration of people at a given position is low,[5] there will be representatives in the legislature who will speak clearly for their interests. For example, if farmers tend to live in districts composed largely of farmers, there will be representatives who will speak for farmers, but if wholesalers are disturbed evenly through the nation there will probably not be any representatives who speak

---

[4] This is $\int Z(w)Y(w)dw$.

[5] That is, if $Z(w_0)$ is low.

clearly for their interests.   However, Key (1964, 143) notes that orga-
nized groups do supplement the system of geographic representation
when no legislator can be relied upon to look out for an interest that
spreads across many districts.

4. Any issue can be removed from national politics by an appropriate construction of district lines.   All that is necessary is to make
each district a miniature version of the national distribution of the
issue dimension.   This will place all the conflict of interest at the district level, and the legislature will consist of representatives from equivalent districts.   This is what Cleisthenes did for the Council of Five
Hundred.   When even a moderate amount of geographic integration
already exists, less arbitrary districts can be constructed which will
absorb most of the conflict of interest at the local level.

5. New parties can arise even if no one's policy preferences
change, provided there is population movement across district lines.

6. Proportional representation tends to leave more conflict of
interest for the legislature to handle than does a system of single member constituencies.   This is so because, unlike a system of single member constituencies (which is what has been considered so far), under
proportional representation not all the conflict of interest within a district is resolved, since several candidates are chosen to go to the
legislature.

The normative criteria that should govern the use of the kind
of "political engineering" discussed in this section are crucial, but these
are for the most part beyond the scope of this study.

D. Theory of Crosscutting and Overlapping Cleavages

THE BASIC PROPOSITION OF THE THEORY

The second application of the idea of conflict of interest at the
societal level is to the theory of crosscutting and overlapping cleavages.
The purpose of this section is to show how the fundamental proposition
in the theory of cleavages can be derived from the definition of societal
conflict of interest and from an application of the general hypothesis
of the theory of conflict of interest.

The literature on cleavages in society is too vast to review in
detail here.   (A recent critical review is offered by Lijphart, 1968,
1–15.)   For present purposes it will suffice to give samples of a few

of the major formulations of the theory. An early formulation of the idea is the one by Edward Ross:

> Every species of social conflict interferes with every other species in society . . . save only when lines of cleavage coincide; in which case they reinforce one another. . . . A society, there-fore, which is ridden by a dozen oppositions along lines running in every direction may actually be in less danger of being torn with violence or falling to pieces than one split along just one line. For each new cleavage contributes to narrow the cross clefts, so that one might say that *society is sewn together* by its inner conflict. (1920, 164–65, quoted in Coser, 1956, 76–77)

More recently, a number of authors have restated this basic idea and have suggested some possible explanations for it. For example, Dahrendorf speaks of the energy an individual devotes to different issues:

> The proposition seems plausible that there is a close positive correlation between the degree of superimposition of conflicts and their intensity. When conflict groups encounter each other in several associations and in several clashes, the energies ex-pended in all of them will be combined and one overriding con-flict of interests will emerge. (1959, 215)

Dahl explains the same proposition by referring to the quality of the relationships between people on different sides of an issue:

> If all the cleavages occur along the same lines, if the same people hold opposing positions in one dispute after another, then the severity of conflicts is likely to increase. The man on the other side is not just an opponent; he soon becomes an enemy. (1967, 277)

With the notable exception of Dahrendorf, most of the authors discussing cleavages do not make a clear distinction between conflict of interest and conflictful behavior. Nevertheless, the basic proposition of the theory of cleavages can easily be stated in these terms.

Basic Proposition of the Theory of Cleavages. If the cleavages in society overlap, then conflictful behavior at the societal level (such as "violence" or "falling to pieces") is relatively likely. Conversely, if the cleavages are crosscutting, relatively little conflictful behavior is expected.

Although much has been written about the usefulness of this theory of cleavages, the basic proposition has never been explained by a derivation in a formal model.   Now that conflict of interest at the societal level has been defined, the task can be undertaken.

The basic proposition of cleavage theory can be derived by introducing social groupings into the spatial model of society.   Suppose one can draw up a list of the social groupings which can be used to help account for the policy preferences of the individuals in the society. Such a list might include Catholics, union members, the elderly, the rich, and so forth.   On a given issue, an individual's preference might be predictable from a knowledge of which of these groupings he belongs to, and how closely he identifies with each one of which he is a part.

An example of an issue is the proper level of Social Security payments (both benefits and taxes).   A person who is typical in every characteristic except that he is Catholic might be expected to support higher payments, while a person who is typical in everything except that he is richer than average might be expected to support lower payments.   This example is illustrated in Figure 7-7.   The new assumption that can be added to the spatial model of society concerns the way in which membership in these social grouping helps determine a person's policy preferences.

The particular form of the new assumption is suggested by the concept of crosspressures.   A person who is both Catholic and rich is expected to take a more moderate view on the issue of Social Security payments than would either a poor Catholic or a rich non-Catholic.   In this sense, the rich Catholic is said to be crosspressured.   As Berelson, *et al.* put it:

> In one sense, the "cross-pressured" people are simply members of separate social groups within which preference distributions are more nearly equal. . . .
>
> Yet, viewing them from the point of view of the total community, they are *in between* the great voting blocs.   (1954, 131)

FIGURE 7-7.   Example of Preferences
on Social Security Payments

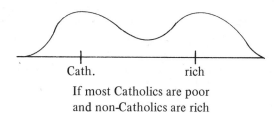

Cath.   rich

If most Catholics are poor
and non-Catholics are rich

FIGURE 7-8.   Overlapping Cleavages
High Conflict of Interest

The assumption this concept suggests is that a person's preferred policy position is the average of the positions of the social groups of which he is a member.   To increase the accuracy of this assumption, the average should be computed as a weighted average with the weights for the groups' influence proportional to the importance of each group to that individual.   Thus membership in latent groups (such as farmers) would be of some predictive value, while membership and identification with a particular association (such as the Grange) might have greater effect on a person's policy preferences.

Some of the hypotheses that have employed the idea of cross-pressures, such as the prediction that cross-pressured people are less likely to vote, have been subject to criticism.   Nevertheless, the assumption that a person's preferred policy can be predicted from the groups to which he belongs seems to be a reasonable one.   This assumption also has the advantage that it can be tested with survey data on an issue-by-issue basis.

Using the spatial model with this new assumption, the basic proposition of cleavage theory can be derived.   The demonstration can be illustrated by the example of the policy issue of Social Security payments, in which being Catholic makes a person want higher payments and being rich makes a person want lower payments.   If most Catholics are poor and most non-Catholics are rich then the religious and economic cleavages overlap for this issue.   There would then be two relatively distinct types of people with quite different policy preferences: the poor Catholics who favor higher payments, and the rich non-Catholics who want lower payments (Figure 7-8).   The resulting bimodal distribution of policy preferences has a relatively high variance, and therefore the societal conflict of interest on the issue is high.

The opposite case occurs when most Catholics are rich and most non-Catholics are poor.   In this case, the religious and economic cleavages are crosscutting and most people are crosspressured.   The policy preferences of most people fall near the middle of the distribution (as shown in Figure 7-9).   Under these circumstances, the distribution has relatively low variance and therefore the societal conflict of interest on this issue is low.

Thus if the religious and economic cleavages overlap societal conflict of interest is high, and if the cleavages crosscut each other, societal conflict of interest is low.   Clearly this result is independent of the specific policy issue and the social cleavages chosen.   It also applies if additional cleavages (such as race, occupation, and religion) are also considered at the same time.   This result can be summarized as follows:

Theorem.   If cleavages overlap (crosscut), societal conflict of interest is high (low).

In the general case of cleavages, the amount of conflict of interest as measured by the variance can be calculated for intermediate cases when the cleavages neither completely overlap or crosscut each other.

The preceding theorem relates cleavages to conflict of interest. The relationship of conflict of interest to conflictful behavior is provided by applying the general hypothesis of the theory of conflict of interest to the societal level: the more societal conflict of interest, the more conflictful behavior in society.   The result is that if cleavages overlap (crosscut), conflictful behavior is high (low) in society.   But this statement is the basic proposition of the theory of cleavages.   The derivation of the basic proposition is recapitulated in the following theorem:

Theorem.   The basic proposition of the theory of cleavages follows from the theory of conflict of interest in four steps:

1. Extension of the definition of conflict of interest in the two-person bargaining game (a definition derived axiomatically in Chapter 2) to derive a definition of conflict of interest in a spatial model of society (a spatial model which assumes that utility loss is proportional to distance).

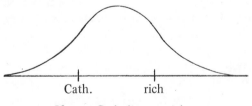

If most Catholics are rich
and non-Catholics are poor

FIGURE 7-9.   Crosscutting Cleavages
Low Conflict of Interest

2. Equivalence of this definition of conflict of interest in society to the variance of the distribution of optimum policy positions.

3. Demonstration of the theorem that overlapping (crosscutting) cleavages means high (low) conflict of interest.

4. Application of the general hypothesis of the theory of conflict of interest to society: the more societal conflict of interest, the more conflictful behavior in society.

The approach used to relate social cleavages to a single issue dimension can also be used to relate several specific issues to a composite dimension such as liberal-conservative or pro-Democrat vs. pro-Republican. Instead of predicting people's positions from their social attributes one would predict positions on the composite dimension from people's positions on the separate issues. The new conclusion that follows from this interpretation of the spatial model is that if the cleavages on specific issues overlap then societal conflict of interest on the composite dimension is high, and if the cleavages on the specific issues crosscut each other then societal conflict of interest is low. As before, the degree of societal conflict of interest can be calculated for the intermediate as well as for these two pure cases.

As is well-known from American survey data (Campbell, *et al.*, 1960, 194–198), New Deal-Fair Deal issues form a Guttman scale as do several foreign policy issues. However, these scales are extremely weak, implying that the cleavages on the specific issues that make up the scales are hardly correlated at all and almost perfectly crosscut one another. This suggests the question of whether any very strong structure exists for American public opinion on policy issues.

The answer, based on 1956 data, is that the strongest composite issue dimension is one which might be called pro- and anti-populism. An extreme pro-populist favors Federal improvement of education, medical care, and job opportunity but is against current tax levels, civil liberties, and foreign involvement (Axelrod, 1967b). Even for this dimension, however, the six specific issues that define it are only weakly related so that the issue cleavages crosscut each other. This empirical finding from 1956, applied to the theorem that crosscutting cleavages mean low societal conflict of interest, provides a partial explanation of why conflictful behavior in the American polity was relatively low.

E. Summary

Concepts closely related to conflict of interest have been invoked throughout the history of Western political thought to deal with the fundamental themes of the common and divergent interests of the members of a political community. This chapter has offered one way in which conflict of interest at the societal level can be specified in a precise way and has applied this formulation to several political problems.

To specify what conflict of interest at the societal level means, a spatial model of society was introduced in which a person's utility loss is proportional to the distance from his optimum position. Then the meaning of conflict of interest between a pair of people in this spatial model was taken directly from the analysis in Chapter 2 for the two-person bargaining game. The societal conflict of interest for a given policy dimension was then defined as the average conflict of interest between two people as each one takes on all the positions in the policy dimension in proportion to the position's frequency in the society, This formulation was shown to have a number of desirable properties, including equivalence to the statistical concept of the variance of a distribution.

Two applications of the formalization of the idea of conflict of interest at the societal level were offered to suggest the usefulness of the concept. The first application was to the subject of apportionment. It was shown that in a given society the conflict of interest could be thought of as existing at either the electoral or legislative levels. The societal conflict of interest could be allocated between these two levels by drawing local political boundaries.

The second application dealt with the theory of crosscutting and overlapping cleavages. The basic proposition of this important theory is that if the various cleavages in a society overlap then the society is in danger of being torn apart, but if they crosscut each other then the society is sewn together. Using the formalization of societal conflict of interest and applying the general hypothesis of conflict of interest theory, this proposition was derived in the context of a spatial model of society.

A good way to extend the conflict of interest analysis of spatial models is to vary the assumptions that are employed. One important line of development, following the lead of such researchers as Black (1958), Davis and Hinich (1966), and Tullock (1967), would be to move from a spatial model with one issue dimension to a multidimensional model. Another step would be to relax the assumptions about the nature of the dimensions themselves to see if any fruitful results could still be derived. A third possibility would be to add political parties as independent actors within the context of a spatial model. The next chapter pursues the last two thoughts by using a very simple model of a one-dimensional policy space to study the coalition process among political parties in parliamentary democracies.

8

Multiparty Coalitions in Parliamentary Democracies

A. Conflict of Interest in Coalitions

COALITIONS IN PARLIAMENTARY DEMOCRACIES

In a parliamentary democracy, political parties contend for legislative seats in a popular election. A cabinet is then formed which seeks to attain a vote of confidence from the legislature. If it is successful, the cabinet and its legislative supporters control the formation and execution of public policy. This situation lasts until the cabinet loses a vote of confidence or until the next general election.

In some parliamentary democracies, such as the United Kingdom, the legislature is usually controlled by a single party. This party can then form a cabinet and govern the nation without having to rely on the support of any other party. However, in other parliamentary democracies, such as Sweden, the Netherlands, France during the Fourth Republic, Italy, and Israel, the legislature usually cannot be controlled by any one party. In order for a cabinet to attain a vote of confidence from the legislature in these countries, the cabinet must be supported by a coalition that includes several different political parties. The question to be examined in this chapter is which coalitions are likely to form and prove durable.

CONTRIBUTION OF CONFLICT OF INTEREST

Predicting which coalition will form can be a difficult matter. For example, if there are seven political parties represented in the legislature (and not infrequently there are even more), then there are 128 possible coalitions. If a simple majority is needed in only one chamber to attain a vote of confidence, then half of these potential coalitions, or 64, are able to govern.[1] With eight parties there are 256 possible coalitions, including 128 coalitions which can govern.

The key point is that not all of the possible coalitions have the same likelihood of forming. The various parties have differing goals, but a given party has goals that are more similar to those of some of the parties than of others. In other words, some potential coalitions have less incompatibility of goals among their members than do others. This of course means that some potential coalitions have less conflict of interest than others.

If some potential coalitions have less conflict of interest among their members than others, perhaps this fact can be used to predict the behavior of the parties in joining and staying in coalitions. The general hypothesis (see Chapter 1) asserts that the more conflict of interest there is, the more likely is conflictful behavior. Sociologists and psychologists have identified many types of conflictful behavior in groups (e.g., Coser, 1956, and M. Deutsch, 1949), and conceivably the general hypothesis could be used to relate conflict of interest in coalitions to each of these types of behavior.

For the present purposes the forms of behavior that are important to predict are the ones with direct political significance. Among the most important political questions about the behavior of parties in a parliamentary democracy are which coalitions they are most likely to form, and which coalitions are most likely to prove durable.

---

[1] The proof is trivial. For n parties there are 2^n potential coalitions, including the coalition with no support and the coalitions with only one member. Each one of these coalitions can be matched with its complement. Either the coalition or its complement has a majority (assuming there are enough seats to make tie votes unlikely). Thus exactly one-half of all coalitions contain a majority of the seats.

The general hypothesis can be reformulated to say that the less conflict of interest there is, the more likely is cooperative behavior. Examples of cooperative behavior are the formation of a coalition and the continued support of an existing coalition.   The formation of a coalition is a form of cooperative behavior among the member parties because by the very act of forming a coalition these parties work together to support a specific cabinet.   The member parties also work together to some extent to cooperate on the passage of agreed-upon items of public policy.   The continued existence of a coalition also requires cooperative behavior because the cabinet falls as soon as it loses a vote of confidence.   These interpretations of political acts provide two predictions which are applications of the general hypothesis:

1. The less conflict of interest there is in a coalition, the more likely the coalition will form.
2. The less conflict of interest there is in a coalition, the more likely the coalition will have long duration if formed.

These predictions are not based on a strong assumption of rationality on the part of the various parties.   Even if people who make the decisions on behalf of the parties do not have a clear conception of the policy goals of the other parties, and even if they do not understand that some coalitions have less conflict of interest than others, the predictions need not fail.   The reason is that negotiations for coalitions that have low conflict of interest will simply be easier to conclude successfully, and hence these coalitions can be expected to be more likely to form—even if the political leaders are not able to identify them beforehand.   Likewise, a coalition with low conflict of interest can be expected to last longer once formed than an average coalition, just because disputes within such a coalition will be easier to resolve.   In a sense, this is a theory of "natural selection" and survival of viable political coalitions.

The next task is to formalize this line of reasoning in such a way that it can be tested.   That task is the subject of the next section. The resulting theory of coalitions based on conflict of interest is then applied to a specific country, Italy, in a specific period, 1953–1968. The success of the theory in predicting the membership and duration of the governmental coalitions is evaluated, the performance of the theory is compared with the performance of earlier coalition theories, and deviant cases are analyzed.   Finally several factors are presented that relate to conflict of interest and might be used to extend the theory.

B. Specification of a Coalition Theory Based on Conflict of Interest

ORDINAL POLICY SPACE

In the preceding chapter (Chapter 7) the concept of a policy space was used in the analysis of conflict of interest in societies. The same concept can also be applied to the study of political parties in legislatures. If the policy preferences of the public can be structured on a left-right dimension, for example, it would not be surprising that the political parties of the same country could also be regarded as occupying positions on a left-right policy dimension.

Fortunately, most of the restrictive assumptions used in the analysis of societal conflict of interest are not needed for a study of conflict of interest in the coalition process. In fact, the most parsimonious of all spatial models is sufficient to develop a testable theory of coalitions based on conflict of interest. All that needs to be assumed is the existence of an ordinal policy dimension, which means that the size of the intervals between positions has no significance. This means that the political parties need only be listed in order (say from left to right). Instead of assuming that utility loss is linear with distance, all that needs to be assumed is the property Black (1958, 7) calls "single-peaked preferences." This is the assumption used by Downs (1957, 115f.) in his spatial model. It simply means that of two policy positions on one side of a political party, the party prefers the closer one. Even the assumption of no anti-system behavior can be dropped because it is not needed for the results that are to be derived from the ordinal model.

This gives the simplest of all policy spaces: a one-dimensional ordinal policy space with ordinal utilities. This spatial model is completely specified by listing the parties in order from one end of the policy dimension to the other.

CONFLICT OF INTEREST IN COALITIONS

Four of the seven requirements discussed in Chapter 4 for a test of a prediction using conflict of interest have now been met for a theory of coalitions. The model of the strategic interaction is merely that a group of political parties controlling enough legislative seats to give a vote of confidence to a cabinet can determine governmental policy. The hypotheses relating conflict of interest to behavior are that the less conflict of interest there is in a coalition, the more likely it will form and the more likely it will be durable if it does form. The possible outcomes are each of the possible combinations of political parties into coalitions. The parties' utilities are incompletely, but sufficiently, specified by their positions in the ordinal policy space.

Now comes the question of how conflict of interest for a coalition can be defined. Since utilities have been specified in only an ordinal fashion for the parties, it is impossible to assign an exact numerical value to the amount of conflict of interest of each potential coalition. However, this is not necessary. It is sufficient to be able to identify the potential coalitions that have comparatively low conflict of interest. If this is done, the predictions that these coalitions are most likely to form and be durable can be tested.

The treatment in Chapter 7 of conflict of interest in spatial models of society provides clues to analyzing conflict of interest in coalitions. Using certain strong assumptions, the first result of that chapter was that conflict of interest in a two-person bargaining game is proportional to the square of the policy distance between the two people. Next, using the same strong assumptions, it was shown that conflict of interest between large numbers of people can be regarded as equivalent to the variance of the distribution of their positions in the policy space. These results employed the assumptions that distance in the policy space can be measured numerically and that utility loss is proportional to policy distance.

What do these results suggest about an ordinal policy space where utility loss can only be said to increase as distance in one direction increases? The answer seems to be that the less dispersion there is in the policy positions of the members of a coalition, the less conflict of interest there is. Of course, the dispersion of a coalition cannot be precisely measured in a strictly ordinal space. Nevertheless, the list of the political parties in order from one end of the policy dimension to the other does provide some information about how dispersed a given coalition is.

For illustration, suppose that the parties are labeled A, B, C, D, E, F, and G in order of their positions from left to right on the policy dimension. In an ordinal policy dimension, the dispersion of the coalition consisting of parties A, B, and C cannot be compared to the dispersion of the coalition consisting of B, C, and D. However, the coalition consisting of the adjacent parties A, B, and C is certain to be less dispersed than the coalition consisting of A, B, and D. For this reason, a coalition consisting of adjacent parties, or a *connected coalition* as it can be called, tends to have relatively low dispersion and thus low conflict of interest for its size.

Of course, the property of a coalition's being connected does not take into account its total spread or dispersion.   The coalition ABC has less dispersion than the coalition ABCD.   Therefore ABC has less conflict of interest than ABCD, even though both coalitions are connected.   Thus the size as well as the connectedness of a coalition affects its conflict of interest.

A third property concerning the strategic capabilities of a coalition can be added to these two properties relating to conflict of interest. The constitution of each parliamentary democracy indicates what a coalition must do to provide a vote of confidence for a cabinet.   Typically, it must obtain a simple majority vote in one or both chambers of the legislature.   A coalition that meets the requirement for providing a vote of confidence can thus control the formation and execution of public policy through its control of the legislative and executive branches of the government.   Such a coalition is called a *winning coalition*.

These three properties of coalitions can be put together to describe the kind of coalitions predicted by a theory based on conflict of interest. The coalition has to be a winning coalition in order to be able to support a cabinet, and it should be connected but not too large in order to have low conflict of interest.   This suggests the following definition:

Definition.   A minimal connected winning coalition (or an *MCW coalition*) is a coalition that is connected (consists of adjacent members); is a winning coalition (can give a cabinet a vote of confidence); and is minimal in the sense that it can lose no member party without ceasing to be connected and winning.

For example, if the seven parties A, B, C, D, E, F, and G are all of equal size and a simple majority is needed for control, then a coalition of any four or more parties is a winning coalition.   There are 64 winning coalitions out of a total of 128 coalitions.[2]   The connected coalitions consist of adjacent members.   There are 28 connected coalitions.[3]   The minimal connected winning coalitions in this example are those coalitions with exactly four adjacent parties.   There are only four of these: ABCD, BCDE, CDEF, and DEFG.   Regardless of the distribution of legislative seats among the parties there are no more than $(n + 1)/2$ minimal connected winning coalitions if there are n parties and if a simple majority of the seats is needed to win.[4]

---

[2] See preceding footnote for proof.

[3] Seven connected coalitions have party A as their leftmost member, six have B as their leftmost member and so on. This gives $7 + 6 + 5 + 4 + 3 + 2 + 1 = 28$.

[4] Here is the proof. Define the median party as the party that has a majority of seats on neither side of it. The median party must be in every

Another formulation of the definition is that a coalition that is connected and winning is also minimal if the exclusion of either of its exterior members leaves a coalition that is no longer a winning coalition.   Thus BCDEF is not a minimal connected winning coalition in the example because the exclusion of either B or F leaves a new coalition that is still winning (and of course it is still connected because only an exterior member was excluded).

Now that the definition of a minimal connected winning coalition has been given, the predictions of the coalition theory based on conflict of interest can be precisely stated.

Hypotheses.   In a parliamentary democracy in which the parties can be placed in a one-dimensional ordinal policy space, minimal connected winning coalitions:

1. are likely to form more often than would be indicated by chance (even compared to just the other winning coalitions), and
2. once formed are likely to be of longer duration than other coalitions.

This leaves only two requirements for a test of a theory using conflict of interest.   The model of strategic interaction has been given; the definition of a minimal connected winning coalition has been derived from conflict of interest considerations; hypotheses relating conflict of interest to behavior have been stated; the possible outcomes have been determined; and the specification of the participants' utilities has been made sufficiently precise by the concept of an ordinal policy space. The two remaining requirements for a test are the observation of behavior and the statistical control of influences other than conflict of interest on behavior.

The observation of the parties' behavior is easy, since the predictions are about which parties support a cabinet and how long a cabinet lasts until it loses a vote of confidence.   These votes are typically a matter of public record in a parliamentary democracy.

The problem of statistical control of influences on behavior other than conflict of interest also presents no problems.   If a sufficiently

---

MCW coalition. Suppose that the median party is the kth from the nearest end. For example, suppose the median party is the third from the left, i.e., party C. Then there are no more than 3 MCW coalitions because no more than one can begin with each of A, B, and C and none can begin with a party to the right of C. In general, if the median party is the kth from the nearest end, there can be no more than k MCW coalitions. The largest k can be is $(n + 1)/2$ which happens when the median party has an equal number of parties on each side of it.

long period of time is chosen, the hypothesis that minimal connected winning coalitions are likely and durable can be statistically tested. If these predictions are confirmed the theory succeeds, otherwise it fails. Thus, if there are other factors such as personal friendships between some of the party leaders which cannot be represented as positions of the parties in the policy space, then these factors will show up as failures of the predictions. Likewise if there are any short-term changes in the relationships between the parties which cannot be treated in terms of the ordinal model and minimal connected winning coalitions, these changes can also appear as failures of the predictions. Since all the requirements of a test of a theory of coalitions based on conflict of interest have been fulfilled, the theory can now be applied to a specific country during a specific time period.

RELATIONSHIP TO OTHER COALITION THEORIES

Before applying the theory to a specific country and performing the actual statistical tests, the relationship between the present theory of coalitions (based on the concept of conflict of interest) and other theories of coalitions should be made clear. There is no need to provide here a comprehensive review of the large amount of theoretical and laboratory work that has been done on coalitions because two excellent critical reviews already exist. The first of these is by Luce and Raiffa (1957, 155–274) and covers roughly the first decade of game theory which began with the work of Von Neumann and Morgenstern (second edition, 1947). A critical review of work on coalitions in the second decade is provided by Leiserson (1966, 38–170).

Although it is not necessary to review here all the contributions of game theory to the study of coalitions, it will be useful to compare the predictions of present theory to those of earlier coalition theories. The four earlier theories that can be applied to the Italian case all assume that the coalition process is a zero-sum game and do not take into account the ideological positions of the parties.

1. Von Neumann and Morgenstern (1947, 420ff.) predict that a coalition will include no parties that are not needed to win. The idea is that in a zero-sum game the winners will not want to share the spoils with any more parties than are necessary.

2. Leiserson's bargaining theory (1968) selects from among those winning coalitions that include no unnecessary parties only those with the fewest number of parties. The idea is that the bargaining process over the formation of a winning coalition is easier if the coalition has only a few parties as members.

3. Riker's basic theory (1962, 32) predicts that of all the winning coalitions only the one of smallest size will form. His idea is that the winning coalition with the least number of seats will be able to give its members the best distribution of the spoils.

4. Riker's modified theory (1962, 77ff.) predicts that since information is not perfect winning coalitions slightly larger than the smallest one may form. For present purposes I will operationalize the modified theory to allow a 5% margin of error, so that any winning coalition with less than 55% of the seats is predicted.

To compare these four theories consider a simple example. Suppose there is a legislature with 31 seats divided among four parties from left to right as follows:

A has 14 seats
B has 3 seats
C has 12 seats
D has 2 seats

If a simple majority is needed to win, the coalition predicted to form by each theory will obviously have at least 16 seats.

Von Neumann and Morgenstern predict that a coalition that forms will not be able to exclude one of its parties and still have a majority. Thus they predict the AB, AC, AD or BCD will form. Leiserson's bargaining theory predicts the coalition with the fewest parties, which in this case is two parties. Thus AB, AC, and AD are his predictions. Riker's basic theory predicts that the coalition will be as small as possible, which in this case means 16 seats, and therefore must be AD. Riker's modified theory allows for winning coalitions with up to 5% of the seats, which in this case is 16 or 17 seats, so AB, AD, or BCD is predicted. None of these theories takes account of the order in which the parties are placed.

In contrast, the theory of coalitions based on conflict of interest predicts that the coalition must be connected. Furthermore, it singles out coalitions that are not able to exclude either of their exterior parties and still have a majority. The only coalitions that fulfill these conditions are AB and BCD.

The coalition theory based on conflict of interest does not assume that the participants are in a zero-sum game. On the contrary, the idea of conflict of interest has been developed precisely to be able to analyze the extent to which situations vary between being partnership games and zero-sum games.

In the ordinal model of policy space, for example, the parties may all have some common interests and some conflicting interests. The assumption used in the present theory of coalitions is that the preferences for public policy of the parties near each other on the policy dimension are similar.   This leads to the idea of a minimal connected winning coalition as a coalition which can be expected to have relatively low conflict of interest.   Thus, unlike the zero-sum theories, the present theory predicts that the policy preferences of a party greatly influence which other parties it is likely to join with in a coalition.   To oversimplify, the present theory denies that coalition politics makes strange bedfellows.

Leiserson (1966) has proposed another coalition theory for non-zero-sum interactions.   This theory assumes that parties search for other parties that are close to them ideologically.   With iterated search procedures used by the parties, coalitions are built up which have minimal ideological diversity.   Ideological diversity is defined in terms of an ideological space similar to the ordinal policy space used in this chapter.   The prediction that coalitions will have minimal ideological diversity is virtually identical to the first hypothesis of the theory of coalitions based on conflict of interest (namely that MCW coalitions are more likely to form than other coalitions).

The theory of coalitions based on conflict of interest is so close to Leiserson's ideological theory that the present theory can be regarded as a derivative of that theory from more fundamental considerations. In other words, the specific form that ideological diversity takes in a spatial model is just another application of the definition of conflict of interest.   The prediction of which coalitions will form is just another application of the general hypothesis for bargaining games.

Leiserson developed his ideological theory of political coalitions after conducting and studying four-person laboratory games.   In the present study, a theoretical analysis of conflict of interest in various contexts (first the bargaining game, later society, and now multiparty coalitions) has provided an alternate route to a virtually identical theory of coalitions.

Needless to say, knowing the nature of Leiserson's theory of ideological diversity aided the development of the present coalition theory based on conflict of interest.   Unfortunately, Leiserson's insightful work contains ambiguities in parts of the theory.   For this reason an exact comparison of his ideological theory and the theory of coalitions based on conflict of interest is not possible at this time.

The conflict of interest approach does have several advantages over the more empirical approach based on laboratory gaming.

1. The conflict of interest approach helps place the coalition theory in a broader context as a special case of a much more general theory.

2. By eliminating some of the *ad hoc* quality of the theory, the conflict of interest approach leads to a more parsimonious model. In particular, the need to assume special search strategies by the participants is replaced by an application of the general hypothesis in the explanation of why certain coalitions are more likely to form than others.

3. The conflict of interest approach suggests an additional hypothesis which goes beyond the prediction of which coalitions will form. This additional hypothesis, of course, is that the MCW coalitions will last longer than other coalitions that form because they are expected to have less internal conflict of interest and hence less internal conflictful behavior. Coalition *formation* has been the main subject of the study of coalition in the game theoretic context (including Leiserson's theory). The conflict of interest approach suggests how the important political question of coalition *maintenance* can also be treated.

The present theory of coalitions based on conflict of interest is inferior in one way to Leiserson's ideological theory. The present theory does not offer any predictions on how the parties in a coalition will distribute among themselves the various posts in the cabinet. Furthermore, the present theory does not directly predict the policies of the coalition government, although knowledge of the government's composition would certainly help in predicting what these policies will be. A comparison of the success of the present theory with the four zero-sum theories will be made in the next section.

C. Application of the Coalition Theory to Italy

THE ITALIAN POLITICAL SYSTEM

The task at hand is to apply the theory of coalitions based on conflict of interest to a specific country during a specific time period. Recent Italian politics have been chosen for the application because there have been a relatively large number of parties and relatively clear positions for these parties in a left-right policy space. This structure allows the use of the one-dimensional ordinal spatial model. The relatively large number of parties in Italy makes the predictions of the theory bold because with many parties only a small proportion of the many possible coalitions are minimal connected winning coalitions.

The Italian Constitution specifies the rule for a coalition to be a winning coalition: to permit a cabinet to win a vote of confidence a coalition must win a majority of votes in both chambers of the Parliament. In fact, the strength of the various parties has been quite similar in both chambers, and no policy conflicts between the chambers have emerged (Kogan, 1962, 93).[5] The political parties themselves are well-disciplined, so that the parties can be regarded as the actors in the coalition process.

The structure of the Italian party system can be viewed in several ways. Sartori (1966, 148) provides a fairly complex description, but most authors (including Sartori) agree that the programs of the various parties make it relatively easy to place them on a single left-to-right dimension. According to Barnes (1966, 304),

> While such a continuum is inadequate for the analysis of many political systems, it does not greatly distort the realities of Italian politics; furthermore, it is a useful way of viewing Italian parties.

Following the consensus among Kogan (1962), Leiserson (1966), Barnes (1966) and Sartori (1966, 140f.), the eight major Italian political parties can be ordered from left to right:[6]

  A. Communist Party
  B. Socialist Party (Nenni Socialists)
  C. Democratic Socialist Party (Saragat Socialists)
  D. Republican Party
  E. Christian Democracy
  F. Liberal Party
  G. P.D.I.U.M. (monarchist party)
  H. Italian Social Movement (neo-Fascist party)

In the first years after World War II the Italian political system was considered fragile and the parties behaved accordingly. The center parties frequently sought more support in the legislature than was absolutely necessary in order to promote the stability of the entire system. This was true during the Constituent Assembly (1946–1948) and during

---

[5] In the interpretation of each theory, the analysis is based on the number of seats in the Chamber of Deputies, but coalitions are considered winning only if they have a majority in both chambers.

[6] See also Note 3 to Table 8-1.

the First Legislature that was elected in an atmosphere of crisis in May, 1948. Not until the Second Legislature was elected five years later could the political parties bargain with each other primarily on the basis of their parliamentary strength. For this reason the period since 1953 has been chosen for analysis.

EMPIRICAL RESULTS

Seventeen cabinets have been formed in Italy from the beginning of the Second Legislature in May, 1953, to the present, January, 1969. The current cabinet is an MCW coalition, but is not included in the analysis of durations because it is still in power.

The allocation of legislative seats resulting from the general elections held every five years beginning in 1953 provides the data needed to determine the minimal connected winning coalitions. During each legislative session there were either two or three minimal connected winning coalitions. Since there are 128 possible winning coalitions with eight parties, the theory of coalitions based on conflict of interest is bold when it singles out from this large number two or three MCW coalitions and predicts that the government will be one of these.

Table 8-1 lists in the first column the minimal connected winning coalitions for each period between elections. It then gives information on each governmental coalition that submitted a cabinet for a vote of confidence. The information provided for each such coalition is the date of the formation of the cabinet, the membership in the coalition, the duration of the coalition in months, and an evaluation of whether the coalition was an MCW coalition and if not, why not.

The first hypothesis about coalitions is that minimal connected winning coalitions are more likely to form than other coalitions. This prediction is confirmed. Of the 17 coalitions, 10 were minimal connected winning coalitions. This is 29 times more often than would be expected by chance even if only winning coalitions are expected.[7] The probability that this result would have been attained by chance is less than one in a thousand.

The second hypothesis about coalitions is that MCW coalitions once formed last longer than other coalitions. This prediction is also confirmed. The MCW coalitions that formed lasted on the average

---

[7] There are an average of 2.6 MCW coalitions at any one time, so the chance of a winning coalition being an MCW coalition is $(2.6)/128 = .020$. The expected number of MCW coalitions is thus only $(.020)(17) = .34$. Ten MCW coalitions occurred, making them $(10)/(.34) = 29$ times more likely than the average winning coalition.

TABLE 8-1
Chronology of Italian Coalitions

MCW Coalitions	Date	Actual Coalition								Duration (months)	Evaluation
		A	B	C	D	E	F	G	H		
OXXXXOOO OOXXXOO OOOOXXXO	7/53	o	o	o	o	X	o	o	o*	½	Not Winning
	8/53	o	o	o	x	X	x	x	o	5	Too Many Supporters
	1/54	o	o	o	x	X	o	o	o	½	Not Winning
	2/54	o	o	X	x	X	X	o	o	17	MCW
	7/55	o	o	X	x	X	X	o	o	22	MCW
	5/57	o	o	o	o	X	o	x	x	13	Not Connected
OOXXXOOO OOOOXXXO	7/58	o	o	X	x	X	o	o	o	6	MCW
	2/59	o	o	o	o	X	x	x	x	13	Too Many Supporters
	3/60	o	o	o	o	X	o	o	x	4	Not Connected
	7/60	o	o	x	x	X	x	o	o	19	Too Many Supporters
	2/62	o	o	X	X	X	o	o	o	16	MCW
OXXXXOOO OOXXXOO OOOOXXXX	6/63	o	x	x	x	X	o	o	o	5	MCW
	12/63	o	X	X	X	X	o	o	o	8	MCW
	7/64	o	X	X	X	X	o	o	o	19	MCW
	2/66	o	X	X	X	X	o	o	o	28	MCW
OOXXXOOO	6/68	o	o	x	x	X	o	o	o	6	MCW
OOOOXXXX	12/68	o	o	X	X	X	o	o	o	—	MCW

*o: Does not support the cabinet.
x: Supports the cabinet, but is not represented in it.
X: Supports the cabinet, and is represented in it.

1. *Sources.* Leiserson (1966, 387–392), Adams and Barile (1961, 87), *Keesing's Contemporary Archives,* Barnes (1966, 435), and the *New York Times.*

2. *Abstentions.* Abstentions were counted as support if and only if the cabinet needed some abstentions to win a vote of confidence and the abstentions were sufficient.

3. *Party Labels.* In October, 1966, the Socialist Party (B) merged with the Democratic Socialist Party (C). This left an existing small group of far-left socialists called the Socialist Party of Proletarian Unity to occupy the first position on the ideological spectrum (A), moving the Communist Party to the second position (B).

4. The coalition of March, 1960 won a vote of confidence only with the help of a few monarchists although most monarchists did not support it. Because of its small size it is counted as a successful prediction by each of the four zero-sum theories.

14 months each compared to only 8 months each for the others. The probability that this result would have been attained by chance is less than one in ten.[8]

During the 15 years under investigation, Italy was governed by a minimal connected winning coalition 70% of the time. This was

[8] This is based on the t-test of the product moment correlation between the duration of the coalitions and their type. It assumes each coalition is an independent event.

TABLE 8-2
Number of Predictions in Each Period

Period	Von Neumann Morgenstern	Leiserson Bargaining	Riker Basic	Riker Modified	Axelrod MCW
1953–1958	7	3	1	12	3
1958–1963	12	3	3	19	2
1963–1968	9	2	2	23	3
1968–1969	10	2	1	24	2
Average	9	3	2	19	3

so despite the fact that of all the potential winning coalitions, only about one in fifty is a minimal connected winning coalition.

COMPARISON TO ZERO-SUM COALITION THEORIES

Compared to the four zero-sum coalition theories, the theory based on conflict of interest is substantially better in predicting which coalitions formed in Italy.   Leiserson's bargaining theory, Riker's basic theory, and the theory based on conflict of interest all made an average of two or three predictions at a time.   However the Von Neumann-Morgenstern theory and the Riker modified theory were much less specific with an average of 9 and 19 predictions respectively.   The theory based on conflict of interest correctly predicted 10 coalitions out of 17.   The other two highly specific theories made one and three correct predictions, while the two less specific theories made three and five correct predictions.   These comparisons are listed in Tables 8-2 and 8-3.

The four theories based on zero-sum reasoning made correct predictions only during the 1958–1963 period.   The two MCW coalitions that formed during this period happened to be among those with the fewest possible number of seats, so they were predicted by the Von Neumann-Morgenstern theory and the Riker theories as well as by

TABLE 8-3
Number of Coalitions Correctly Predicted

Period	Actual Number Formed	Von Neumann Morgenstern	Leiserson Bargaining	Riker Basic	Riker Modified	Axelrod MCW
1953–1958	6	0	0	0	0	2
1958–1963	5	3	1	3	5	2
1963–1968	4	0	0	0	0	4
1968–1969	2	0	0	0	0	2
Total	17	3	1	0	5	10

the theory based on conflict of interest.   The other winning coalition
that was as small as possible also occurred once although it was not
connected.   In addition, Riker's modified theory scored two more suc-
cesses with connected winning coalitions that had less than 55% of
the seats but did not need both of their exterior members.

In the other three periods, the theory based on conflict of interest
correctly predicted 8 of the 12 coalitions that formed, while the other
four theories predicted none at all.   All the winning coalitions in these
years contained parties that were not needed for a majority, so both
the Von Neumann-Morgenstern theory and Leiserson's bargaining theory failed.   All the winning coalitions in these years also exceeded
55% of the seats so both of Riker's theories failed.   The zero-sum
theories failed to predict that if two parties are in a coalition all the
parties between them must also be in the coalition.   They also failed
to predict that the party which has a majority on neither side of it
(which happens always to have been the Christian Democrats) must
be in the coalition.

The theory based on conflict of interest does at least twice as
well as any of the four theories based on the zero-sum assumption.
The comparison tends to reinforce the point that in studying a situation
that is inherently non-zero-sum, the application of a zero-sum theory
may not be very successful.   On the other hand conflict of interest
analysis is designed for the study of non-zero-sum interactions, and
the coalition theory based on conflict of interest does indeed make
better predictions.

DEVIANT CASE ANALYSIS

An examination of the Italian coalitions that were not minimal
connected winning coalitions is instructive.   Table 8-4 lists the various

TABLE 8-4
Coalitions in Italy (1953–1968) by Types

	Number of Occurrences	Average Duration (Months)	Percent of Total Months
Not Winning	2	$\frac{1}{2}$	1%
Winning But Not Connected	2	9	9%
Connected and Winning But Not Minimal			
Cabinet Too Inclusive	0	—	0%
Too Many Supporters	3	9	20%
Minimal Connected Winning	10	14	70%
	17	12	100%

types of coalitions and gives the number of times each occurred, the average duration of the type, and the percentage of time the type existed.

The most drastic type of departure from an MCW coalition was a coalition that was not even winning. Coalitions that could not win a vote of confidence were rare and of short duration, as would be expected. Both occurrences of this type lasted only about a fortnight until a winning coalition could be formed. Altogether only one percent of the total period was taken by these non-winning coalitions.

A coalition that was winning but not connected occurred only twice among the seventeen coalitions in the period. The cause of the first of these unusual coalitions (that did manage to last for thirteen months until the next general election in the summer of 1958) was apparently that two members of the previous coalition (the Democratic Socialists, C, and the Liberal Party, F) had unrealistically high aspirations for cabinet positions. Therefore the central member of the old coalition (the Christian Democracy, E) accepted the support of the two right wing parties. However, when election gains for the Christian Democrats allowed them to rule with only the help of the Democratic Socialists, these two parties supported by the Republicans promptly formed a minimal connected winning coalition. The second disconnected coalition occurred in March–April, 1960, when no party but the neo-Fascists (H) voted for a cabinet composed solely of Christian Democrats. The Christian Democrats were so embarrassed that the government resigned three days later. Four months were needed to form another government. Between them, the two disconnected coalitions lasted an average of 9 months and occupied 9% of the total months of the period.

Of the coalitions that were connected and winning but not minimal, two types can be distinguished. The first type has more than the necessary number of parties represented in the cabinet. The second type is not minimal only because one or more of the parties that voted for the cabinet in the original vote of confidence were not needed to make the coalition be connected and winning.

Cabinets that contained more parties than were necessary never occurred in this period. It is interesting that several coalitions of this type did occur in the years immediately after World War II. During that period the heritage of the War made national unity especially difficult and extremely desirable. Thus the center parties had a major interest in extending membership in the cabinet as widely as possible. This unusual aspect of the parties' preferences during the years after the War is not reflected in the ordinal spatial model, but it could conceivably be incorporated into a more comprehensive model of the parties' preferences.   If this were done, the results might well show that these "unnecessarily" inclusive cabinets still had very low conflict of interest due to the unusually large common interest of most of the parties in national unity.

The other type of coalition that was connected and winning but not minimal was one that had no unneeded parties in the cabinet, but did have unnecessary support from parties not represented in the cabinet.   Such coalitions occurred three times and lasted an average of nine months each, accounting for 20% of the total months of the period.

This type of large coalition, with unneeded support from parties not in the cabinet, may actually have been strategically similar to a minimal connected winning coalition.   After all, the extra supppporters may not even have been wanted by the other members of the coalition.   These extra supporters may have voted for the cabinet out of fear of a worse coalition, rather than because of some reward promised by the other members of the coalition.   In other words, a coalition that appeared to have unnecessary supporters may actually have been an MCW coalition that had also picked up some unsolicited support of other parties.   Thus the coalitions that are connected and winning but have too many supporters outside the cabinet can be regarded as "almost" MCW coalitions.

The voting record is not sufficient evidence to decide which parties' votes were solicited and which were not.   If further evidence were available that identified these three "almost" MCW coalitions as really just MCW with unsoliciated supporters, then the total duration of coalitions that were essentially minimal connected winning coalitions would increase from 70% to 90% of the months of the 1953–1968 period in Italy.   (See Figure 8-1.)

The examination of the types of coalitions that were not MCW coalitions has shown that none of these types occurred nearly as frequently as MCW coalitions, nor had duration as long as the MCW coalitions.   The coalitions that were not winning were of course rare and brief.   Of the two coalitions that were winning but not connected,

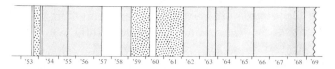

FIGURE 8-1.   Time Line of Italian Coalitions
(Shaded areas: MCW coalitions)
(Dotted areas: "almost" MCW coalitions)

one was probably the result of unrealistically high aspirations and was promptly re-evaluated after the next general election.   The other was such an embarrassment to the members of the cabinet that they resigned almost immediately.   Connected coalitions with unnecessary members in the cabinet never occurred during this period although they were common in the early years after World War II.   The three coalitions that drew unneeded support from parties not in the cabinet might actually have been MCW coalitions whose extra supporters were entirely unsolicited.   Additional evidence is needed, however, to test this possibility.

The examination of the coalitions which were not minimal connected winning coalitions has thus suggested several factors that might be built into a more comprehensive theory of coalitions based on conflict of interest.   Two of these factors are the possibility of low conflict of interest between the parties in times of national emergency and the possibility of parties' unsolicited support to what would otherwise be a minimal connected winning coalition.

D. Some Possible Extensions of the Theory

Three other ways in which the theory of coalitions based on conflict of interest can be extended are:

1. *Consideration of intraparty factions.*   When there are several MCW coalitions, consideration of the relative strengths of the factions within the parties may be useful in specifying the unique prediction of which MCW coalition will form.   One way of doing this is suggested by DeSwaan (forthcoming) in his proposition that each party tries to form a coalition with parties on both sides of itself so that it is near the center of the coalition.   This can be interpreted as a desire to minimize conflict of interest with the anticipated policy decisions of the coalition.   DeSwaan's proposition also suggests that a large diffuse center party (such as the Christian Democracy in Italy) will tend to join parties to its left when its left wing is strong and to its right when its right wing is strong.

2. *Use of complex policy spaces.*   Extending the theory to a multidimensional policy space can be done in a straightforward manner.[9]   Other structures, such as rings, could also be employed where appro-

---

[9] In a multidimensional ordinal spatial model convexity is the generalization of the property of connectedness. In an appropriate multidimensional *cardinal* model, a unique prediction could be made by specifying the winning coalition with the smallest set theoretic diameter.

priate (e.g., on the three-way division in the Netherlands between Protestant, Catholic, and nonreligious parties, or in countries where the two extreme parties are quite close to each other in their policy preferences). A closer approximation to reality is purchased with the sacrifice of some parsimony in the model when these more complex structures are used.

3. *Prediction of electoral coalitions.* In some countries (such as France) parties have an incentive to form coalitions in presenting lists of parliamentary candidates to the voters. A theory closely related to Leiserson's ideological theory has already been developed by Rosenthal (1967) for the *post hoc* explanation of electoral coalitions in France.

E. Summary

This chapter has applied the tools of conflict of interest analysis to develop a theory of coalitions in parliamentary democracies. Using the simplest possible spatial model (a one-dimensional ordinal model), it was shown that coalitions with low conflict of interest can be expected to be connected and small. This led to the definition of a minimal connected winning coalition as one composed of adjacent parties in the policy space and capable of winning a vote of confidence for a cabinet, but not able to lose any of its member parties without ceasing to be connected and winning.

The general hypothesis for conflict of interest was then invoked to suggest two predictions for a theory of coalitions. These predictions are (1) that minimal connected winning coalitions are more likely to form than other coalitions, and (2) that once formed they are likely to last longer than other coalitions.

This theory of coalitions based on conflict of interest considerations is very similar to the ideological theory developed by Leiserson (1966), but has three advantages over that theory. First, it is derived from very fundamental considerations (i.e., from conflict of interest analysis), thereby placing it in a broader context as a special case of a much more general theory. Second, it is much more parsimonious. Third, the conflict of interest approach suggests the additional prediction of longer duration as well as higher frequency of formation for the specified coalitions. The present theory of coalitions based on conflict of interest is inferior in the sense that it does not predict the allocation of cabinet positions among the member parties of the coalition.

The two predictions of the theory of coalitions based on conflict of interest, that minimal connected winning coalitions are likely to form and be durable, were tested with the record of coalitions in Italy during the period 1953–1968. During this period, seventeen coalitions formed, of which ten were minimal connected winning coalitions. The results confirm the predictions. Minimal connected winning coalitions occurred twenty-nine times more often than would be expected by a random selection of winning coalitions. The MCW coalitions formed lasted on the average of 14 months compared to only 8 months each for the others. The first result had less than one chance in a thousand of occurring by chance, and the second less than one chance in ten. Even though there were only two or three possible minimal connected winning coalitions at any one time (out of 128 possible winning coalitions), Italy was ruled by a minimal connected winning coalition for 70% of the months in the period.

A comparison of the present theory to four earlier zero-sum coalition theories showed that the non-zero-sum characteristic of Italian politics needs to be taken into account. The theory based on conflict of interest correctly predicted ten of seventeen coalitions, while none of the zero-sum theories correctly predicted more than five. This result occurred despite the fact that two of the zero-sum theories made on the average more than three times as many predictions as the theory based on conflict of interest.

An examination of the types of coalitions that formed but which were not minimal connected winning coalitions showed that none of these types occurred nearly as frequently as the minimal connected winning coalitions, or lasted as long as the minimal connected winning coalitions. This examination of deviant cases highlighted several factors that might be built into a more comprehensive theory of coalitions based on conflict of interest, especially the possibility of low conflict of interest between the parties in times of national emergency and the possibility of parties' unsolicited support to what would otherwise be a minimal connected winning coalition.

Several other extensions of the theory of coalitions based on conflict of interest were also mentioned, including the consideration of intra-party factions, the use of complex policy spaces, and the prediction of electoral coalitions.

POSTSCRIPT:
RECENT EVENTS IN ITALY

Events in Italy since this chapter was written provide interesting illustrations of the use of the coalition theory based on conflict of interest.

In August, 1969, a new government was formed after a right wing group split off from the Socialist Party to establish a new party called the Unified Socialist Party (see also note 3, page 178). The new party's ideological position is presumably just to the right of the Socialists. The theory has no difficulty dealing with this split even though it is a major change in the Italian political scene. The theory predicts that with the current distribution of seats, the new government should consist of the Christian Democrats supported by one of the following groups:

1. the Socialists, Unified Socialists, and Republicans, or
2. the Unified Socialists, Republicans, and Liberals, or
3. the Liberals, monarchists, and neo-Fascists.

The government that actually formed was identical to the first one listed above, except that the tiny Republican Party, which is nestled between the Unified Democrats and the Christian Democrats, abstained rather than voted for the new government.

This result must be counted as a failure of the theory even though the Republicans have only 1 percent of the votes in the Chamber of Deputies, were not needed for a majority, and did not vote against the government. This narrow failure of the theory is the price one pays for specificity in predictions.

Most observers expect a new government to be formed after the local elections of November, 1969. If so, the hypothesis about membership of the present coalition will still be wrong, but the hypothesis about the short duration of an unconnected coalition will be correct. In fact, the Republicans may have abstained just because they expected a short life for the coalition.

For the next government, the theory predicts that with the current legislative strengths of the parties, one of the three coalitions listed above will form. Many observers cite the possibility of very different combinations next time, so Italy will undoubtedly remain an interesting test case for the theory of minimal connected winning coalitions.

October, 1969

9

Conclusion:
The State of the Art

A. Common Sense Revisited

This study began with the common sense idea that other things being equal, the more conflict of interest there is, the more likely is conflictful behavior. It then set forth some properties that a formal definition of conflict of interest should have in one particular context. These properties might also be regarded as common sense. The rest of the study was largely an elaboration on these two steps. This might suggest the question of whether anything was accomplished that was not merely a product of everyday common sense.

Karl Deutsch (1959) has identified three difficulties with unaided common sense. First, a proposition widely regarded as common sense may in fact be untrue. Second, what is regarded as common sense may be a matter of changing fashions. Finally, and perhaps most important, the maxims of common sense may be contradictory. For example, we are told that "opposites attract," and also that "birds of a feather flock together."

Thus it may be just common sense that other things being equal, the more conflict of interest there is, the more likely is conflictual behavior. On the other hand, even those who specialize in the study of conflict have rarely made explicit the distinction between the state of conflict of interest and the resultant conflictful behavior. Making this distinction explicit suggested the basic theme of this study which in turn served as a working hypothesis: a suggestion about how the investigation might proceed.

The definition of conflict of interest in the bargaining game was derived from a list of properties the definition should fulfill. These properties may be one version of common sense, but other versions might suggest different or even contradictory properties. The theorem that the proposed list is satisfied by one and only one procedure for measuring conflict of interest in the bargaining game could hardly have been seen with unaided common sense. The resulting procedure provides a definition of conflict of interest that is certainly intuitively justifiable, but again it is unlikely that unaided common sense could have discovered this one definition and rejected all others.

Von Neumann and Morgenstern (1947, 7f.) are also concerned with the relationship between theory and common sense. They point out that the first uses of a theory are necessarily to elementary problems for which the result is not in doubt and no theory is actually needed. At this first stage the application serves to corroborate the theory. The next stage occurs when the theory is applied to somewhat more complicated situations, and here the theory and application corroborate each other. Beyond this they see the field of real success: genuine prediction by theory.

Common sense can be transcended. The purposes of this study have been to specify one version of common sense, to formalize that version, to develop tools of analysis and measurement, to use these tools to relate quite different political problems to each other, to extend the procedures to cover a broader and broader range of topics, to try to explain diverse political processes in terms of common principles about conflict of interest so that the persuasiveness of each explanation is reinforced by the others, to formulate falsifiable predictions, to test and evaluate these predictions, and to assess the state of the art of the whole effort.

What remains is the assessment of the state of the art of conflict of interest analysis. The purpose is to present a functional overview of what has been done in this study so the work that remains to be done on conflict of interest can begin to be mapped out.

Rather than discuss the application of conflict of interest to one topic after another, the treatment here will be by functional category: the definition of conflict of interest, the tools of analysis, the techniques of measurement, the employment of predictions, the arenas of applications, and the issues of policy. The results of the previous chapters will be listed when appropriate (with reference to chapter and section in parentheses), but no attempt will be made to repeat the development of arguments since most of the chapters have a summary of their own.

B. Definition of Conflict of Interest

This study started with an informal definition of conflict of interest as the state of incompatibility of the goals of two or more actors (Chapter 1, section A). By developing a list of desirable properties for conflict of interest in the so-called bargaining game (2B), a formal definition was derived for conflict of interest in that kind of strategic interaction. It was shown that this definition (representable as the ratio of two areas) was the only one which satisfied the five desirable properties (2C) and was in fact justifiable on intuitive grounds as well (2D). Turning from bargaining to the problem of collective action, the definition of conflict of interest was generalized to cover the game known as the Prisoner's Dilemma (3A).

The bargaining game and the Prisoner's Dilemma are two of the most important examples of abstract strategic interactions. The ability to treat them in terms of conflict of interest has provided a narrow but well-placed base upon which a great amount of model building can be done.

Some further generalizations proved easy to make once the basic definitions were established for these two types of games. The three-person equivalent of the Prisoner's Dilemma was easily treated (3B), and it was shown how any number of players could be handled in a conflict of interest analysis of either the n-person Prisoner's Dilemma or the n-person bargaining game (3B). Conflict of interest was further generalized to treat whole societies in the context of a spatial model of policy preferences, with conflict of interest turning out to be equivalent under certain strong assumptions to the variance of the distribution of policy preferences (7B). This in turn suggested how the n-actor coalition process could be treated in a spatial model with weak assumptions, either one-dimensionally (8B) or multidimensionally (8D).

These types of strategic interaction, taken together, constitute only a tiny part of the realm of possible interactions. For example, they do not begin to cover the case of the players' utilities interacting with each other (Valavanis, 1958), nor the case of the players' ability to deceive each other.

How can conflict of interest between people be usefully defined in a formal manner for all types of strategic interactions? So far this is an unanswered question. What is now known is that a useful definition of conflict of interest exists for a few specific types of games, and there are a few properties which should presumably be satisfied by any definition of conflict of interest for other types of games (4A). What is not yet known is how specific formal definitions of conflict of interest can be generalized to cover wide classes of games. If not all types of games can be covered, of considerable interest would be the extent and reasons for this restriction, and whether a concept broader than conflict of interest could prove useful in the analysis of the games that do not have a simple kind of conflict of interest between their players.

C. Tools of Analysis

This study has used many different types of analyses in an effort to investigate many different types of political processes. Sometimes the analysis took the form of a mathematical derivation in order to spell out the implications of certain assumptions. This was done for the derivation of the definition of conflict of interest in the bargaining game (2C). It was also done in the derivation of the fundamental proposition of the theory of cleavages (7D). But sometimes a historical treatment or detailed case study was used when the complexity of the situation made these methods more appropriate, as in the study of the Congressional conference committee (5B and 5D). Sometimes the purpose was to test predictions, as for the Prisoner's Dilemma (3B) and for coalitions (8). But sometimes it was to provide a conceptual framework in which the relevant questions could be asked, as for the multilevel decisionmaking process in bureaucracies (6). Sometimes the purpose was to provide new justifications for old theories, as for the theory of cleavages (7D). But sometimes it was to present new problems, such as the allocation of electoral and legislative conflict of interest (7C).

These diverse types of analyses have suggested a wide variety of specific tools for use in the study of conflict of interest.

Consider, for example, the question of how the essentially static concept of conflict of interest can be related to the many roles that time plays in strategic interactions. Quite a variety of approaches have been used in this study to treat the question of time. The effects of the history of the interaction on current behavior can be partially explained by how much conflict of interest there is, as was shown with empirical data on the Prisoner's Dilemma (3B). The amount of conflict of interest in a bargaining game can, if necessary, be regarded as a direct function of the length of time it takes to reach an agreement (5D). The time horizon of the participants can also be treated as a variable that affects conflict of interest (5D). A complex strategic interaction can be broken down into sequences of separate games or even games within games (6). Also treatable is the impact of the scarcity of a decisionmaker's time (6F). Perhaps the rise of some new parties could be partially explained by changes in the geographic distribution of people with fixed preferences (7D). Certainly the polarization of a society over time can be treated in terms of societal conflict of interest (7A).

Another set of tools was developed for alleviating the need to determine the precise utility to the players of the no agreement point in a bargaining game. One method is to use the concept of absolute conflict of interest, which is often less sensitive to the location of the no agreement point than the more basic type of (relative) conflict of interest that has been used throughout this study (4B). Another method is to state the amount of conflict of interest as a function of the utility of the no agreement point (5D). The use of spatial models of policy preferences is another way to alleviate the need to determine the no agreement point because with spatial models certain results can be derived with only weak assumptions about the location of the no agreement point (7B and 8B).

The most widely used set of tools in this study has been based on a geometric interpretation of conflict of interest. For example, in the bargaining game the lowering of the player's maximum demand, the introduction of new feasible agreements, and a change in the no agreement point are all easy to evaluate in geometric terms (2E). Parametric interpretations of the algebraic formulas for conflict of interest provide another set of analytic tools. Examples include the analysis of the roles of the various Prisoner's Dilemma parameters, such as the temptation to defect (3B); the comparison of different indices of behavior (3B); and the exploration of the implications for behavior in specific political arenas, such as the behavior of high-level officials in bureaucracies (6D).

The alternative types of conflict of interest (defined in 4B) have also been useful tools of analysis. Although the primary concept is relative, absolute conflict of interest also contributed to the study of the Congressional conference committee (5D). Although the extent to which conflict of interest is informed or uniformed in an implicit consideration throughout the study, it is explicit in such topics as the role of certain salutory beliefs of bureaucrats (6F). Although the basic concept is total, restricted conflict of interest has been useful in the analysis of the separate stages of the multilevel decisionmaking process in bureauracies (6D), and the conflict of interest that is internal to a coalition (8A).

There is no need to list here every type of analytic tool used in this study, but perhaps a few more examples will be useful in illustrating the range of applicability of these tools to the analysis of conflict of interest. Considerations of both money and personal prestige can be treated (5D), as can the compounding of many issues into a single dispute in both the legislative arena (5D), and society at large (7D). The strategic differences between the right to be consulted and full veto power can also be treated (6E), as can certain aspects of the more general problem of the power relationships between parts of an integrated system, such as a large bureaucracy (6F). Even a limited comparison and evaluation of different personal operating styles is feasible (6F).

In general, the development and application of tools for conflict of interest analysis can proceed at two levels. The first level is that of the abstract strategic interaction. Analytic tools at this level can find applications in a wide variety of arenas. Examples are the geometric and parametric forms of analysis of conflict of interest. The second level is that of the tools that are suggested by the specific context of the unique strategic interaction of a given political arena. An example is the penalty vector that is invoked when a bureaucrat cannot resolve an issue at his own level (6B). For both levels, it is quite clear that this study has hardly begun to explore the range of tools that are potentially available for the analysis of conflict of interest.

D. Techniques of Measurement

The use of the concept of conflict of interest poses no problems of measurement beyond the problems that exist for any other type of game theory study. The measurement problems are severe, but they are not unique to the conflict of interest approach. A complete test of a prediction requires measurement or control of the utility schedules of the players, the range of feasible outcomes, the actual behavior, and any influences on behavior which are not taken into account by the game theory formulation or the experimental design. Of course conflict of interest does not have to be measured directly because it can be calculated from the utilities of the players for a given type of strategic interaction.

In assessing the techniques of measurement employed in this study, it should be kept in mind that for many purposes precise measurement is not required.   This is especially true when the purpose of the analysis is the elucidation of the nature of a political process rather than the confirmation of a theoretical prediction about the process.   However, to pose the measurement problems in their most severe form, this section concentrates mainly on the techniques that can be used in the testing of predictions.

The greatest measurment problem, and perhaps the greatest problem of all in the application of a game theory approach, is the determination of the players' utilities.   The variety of techniques that have been used in this study to deal with the determination of utility schedules can be placed into three categories: the controlled setting of utilities, the direct measurement of utilities, and the weakening of the requirements for knowledge of utilities.   The first method, the controlled setting of utilities, is possible in the context of laboratory gaming.   In testing the predictive value of the definition of conflict of interest for the Prisoner's Dilemma, use of prior research in laboratory gaming was a very convenient method of resolving the problem of measuring utilities (3B).

The second approach to the problem of measuring utilities is the direct one.   Several procedures are available including use of a lottery or interviews, and inference from objective criteria or past behavior (4A).   For example, in the case study of the appropriations controversy of 1962 in the Congressional conference committee, objective criteria, the participants' own announcements, and past behavior were all used to help estimate utilities (5D).   An appendix to the same chapter described how interviews with the participants or their staffs could be used to yield more accurate estimates of utilities.   For the analysis of conflict of interest at the societal level, survey research can provide the interview data required to determine the distribution of policy preferences (7B, 7C, and especially 7D).

The third approach to the problem of utility measurement is to weaken the measurement requirements.   Often utilities need not be determined precisely, but only to a rank order.   Thus for example, if the no agreement point in a bargaining game becomes worse for one player than it was before, conflict of interest tends to decrease. Statements of this form, requiring only ordinal utility measurements, are frequently sufficient to pose testable propositions (2E, 3B, 4A). Another way of weakening the requirements for utility measurement is to use a spatial model of policy preferences.   Even a spatial model with strong assumptions eases the measurement problems considerably because only an individual's optimum policy position rather than his entire utility schedule, has to be determined (7B).   Combining ordinal utilities with a weak one-dimensional model of policy preferences, as was done for the Italian political parties (8C), reduces the problem of utility measurement to almost negligible proportions. All that is then needed is a list of the parties from left to right along the single dimension.

Another measurement problem is the determination of the range of possible outcomes. Two specific techniques have been developed to deal with it when the number of possible outcomes becomes inconveniently large. One technique that had been applied to the bargaining game is a procedure to derive a good approximation of the amount of conflict of interest in a given situation with knowledge of only a few of the many possible outcomes (4A). Another procedure is to treat the many possible outcomes as just different combinations of a few basic elements. An example of the latter procedure was presented in the Appendix to Chapter 5: the many possible compromise bills on a subject in Congress can be treated as different combinations of the relatively few elementary clauses in dispute.

In the measurement of behavior, observation of significant behavior is often easy. The problem frequently comes in the interpretation, or coding, of the various forms of behavior in terms of relevant categories. Sometimes even the coding is not difficult, provided the specific type of behavior that is predicted is readily identifiable. This is the case for laboratory games (3B); agreements on bills in the Congressional conference committee (Appendix to 5); the movement of issues from one level of a bureaucracy to another (6B); and the votes of the parties in a public vote of confidence in support of a cabinet in parliamentary democracy (8C). Sometimes the coding of behavior is not as easy. The complex tactics used in the intricate Congressional conference appropriations dispute of 1962 (5D) were not always easy to classify. Likewise the general level of conflictful behavior in a given society at a given time is not always simple to evaluate except in extreme cases. However, examination of extreme cases is often suggestive: the greatest growth in the institutional strength of the Congressional conference committee system characterized the very conflictful period just before the Civil War (5D); the reapportionment plan of Cleisthenes greatly alleviated the danger from regionally based factions in Athens in the sixth century B.C. (7C); and the lack of overlapping issue cleavages marked the relatively calm mid-1950's in the United States.

Finally, there is the question of measuring or controlling for influences on behavior other than those taken into account by the game theory formulation used in a conflict of interest analysis. Formally, the general hypothesis of conflict of interest involves an assumption of "holding other things equal" known as the *ceteris paribus* assumption. This assumption can be met in several different ways (4A). For example, the predictions can be formulated in such a way that a failure of the *ceteris paribus* assumption shows up as a failure of the predictions (8C). Another useful technique is the analysis of deviant cases even when the predictions are confirmed for the range of events examined (8C).

In this study the arenas selected for examination have been chosen on the basis of three criteria: a) the political activity is significant in its own right, b) the process could be represented in one of the forms for which a justifiable definition of conflict of interest could be derived, and c) the measurement problems are not overwhelming. The measurement problems did in fact limit the type of analysis in this study to something less than a statistical test of predictions in most cases. In only two cases were data available for a statistical test: the laboratory gaming of the Prisoner's Dilemma (3B) and the coalition process in parliamentary democracies (8C).

Future advances in techniques of measurements will undoubtedly be a major factor in the eventual progress (or lack of it) not only of conflict of interest analysis but of all other applications of game theory as well. The single greatest problem of measurement is the determination of the utility schedules of the players. Perhaps research in cognitive processes will help bypass the difficulty of directly determining preferences by specifying how preferences are formed in the first place. Among the topics in exploration of the process of utility formation are learning, persuasion, group identification, friendship, and changes of utility due to the strategic interaction itself.

E. Predictions

The general hypothesis of this study is that, other things being equal, the more conflict of interest there is, the greater the likelihood of conflictful behavior (1B). For example, in bargaining games this gives the prediction that the more conflict of interest there is, the greater the likelihood that no agreement will be reached between the players (2D). Specific applications include the prediction that bills with high conflict of interest between Senate and House conferees are more likely to die in conference (Appendix to 5), and that issues with high conflict of interest between bureaucrats in different agencies are less likely to be resolved at a low level in the bureaucracy (6B).

As applied to the Prisoner's Dilemma, the general hypothesis yields the basic prediction that the more conflict of interest, the greater the likelihood the players will defect rather than cooperate with each other. Closely related applications of the general hypothesis can also be used to make predictions about (a) the effect of the previous move, and (b) behavior in the three-person equivalent of the Prisoner's Dilemma. Fortunately, there exists a suitable body of laboratory data on the Prisoner's Dilemma by Rapoport and his colleagues which allowed a test of the basic prediction and the variations on it (3B). Each of the following results has been confirmed by the empirical data and has less than one chance in eighty of occurring by chance (except number 3, which has less than one in twenty-five):

1. The more conflict of interest there is, the more likely a player will defect in a Prisoner's Dilemma.
2. The likelihood of defection is affected in the manner predicted by an application of the general hypothesis to the formula for conflict of interest; it increases (1) with a decrease in the reward for cooperation or the sucker's payoff and (2) with an increase in the temptation to defect or the punishment for failure to cooperate.
3. The effect of the previous move depends on conflict of interest in the predicted manner, e.g., the more conflict of interest, the more "perfidy," "vengefulness," "greed," and "distrust." A corollary of this result is that learning to cooperate is harder in a high conflict of interest situation.
4. In the three-person equivalent of the Prisoner's Dilemma, the more conflict of interest that exists, the greater the likelihood of defection. The proposed definition of conflict of interest is a better predictor of actual behavior than any previously proposed index for the three-person equivalent to the Prisoner's Dilemma.

Another way of stating the main results is that the rank order correlation coefficient between the conflict of interest and the percentage of defection for the two- and three-person Prisoner's Dilemma is .86 and .78 respectively.

To demonstrate that predictions about the complex world of politics could also be tested, a theory of coalitions was developed from the idea of conflict of interest. Using an ordinal spatial model of policy preferences of the political parties, a specific type of coalition, called a minimal connected winning coalition, was identified (8B). Once again applying the general hypothesis, it was predicted that these minimal connected winning coalitions would be more likely to form in support of a cabinet in a parliamentary democracy, and once formed would be of longer duration than other coalitions. These predictions were tested with the record of the seventeen coalitions in Italy from 1953–1968:

1. Minimal connected winning coalitions occured 29 times more often than would be expected from a random selection of coalitions that could have won a vote of confidence.

2. The minimal connected winning coalitions lasted on the average of 14 months, compared to 8 months for other coalitions that formed.

The coalition theory based on conflict of interest made at least twice as many correct predictions of Italian coalitions as any of the four previously proposed zero-sum coalition theories.

The combination of high likelihood and comparatively long duration meant that in the period under investigation, Italy was governed by a minimal connected winning coalition 70% of the time. This was so despite the fact that of all the possible winning coalitions, only about one in fifty was a minimal connected winning coalition.

What should be done to advance the predictive value of the concept of conflict of interest? The following are five suggestions for future work.

1. *Test with more data.* Confronting new applications of the general hypothesis with empirical data is certain to be a worthwhile activity. Several types of data are potentially available. There are laboratory experiments, either ones that have already been conducted which vary the amount of conflict of interest (but unfortunately these are quite rare); or (hopefully) new experiments that are inspired by the availability of precise definitions of conflict of interest for various kinds of games. More data from the political world should also be used. The theory of coalitions based on conflict of interest could be tested with the historical record of a number of different countries, and the suggestions for a test of the bargaining process of the Congressional conference committee (Appendix to 5) could also be tried. The further generalization of conflict of interest to more types of games and the refinement of measurement techniques will open up new arenas for empirical testing. In the meantime, case studies can be undertaken to confront the abstract propositions about conflict of interest with the complexities of the political world.

2. *Specify the general hypothesis more precisely.* The general hypothesis (that other things being equal, the more conflict of interest

there is, the more likely is conflictful behavior) is appropriately abstract, but it could still be made more precise. For example, it begs a number of questions concerning the effects of inaccurate perceptions of the players. Some of these questions have already been considered, but not all have been adequately answered (1B on the assumption of awareness of conflict of interest, 2E on the effects of misunderstanding of outcomes, 4B on informed versus uninformed conflict of interest, 5C on the assumption of perfect information, and 8C on the possibility of unrealistic aspirations).

3. *Define conflictful behavior more precisely.* This study has managed to side-step this issue by only trying to predict the likelihood of certain selected acts that were either obviously conflictful (such as defection in the Prisoner's Dilemma) or obviously the opposite of conflictful (such as forming a coalition). A more subtle treatment of behavior in a given arena would start from a specification of an entire dimension of acts—from very cooperative to very conflictful—and then predict that movement along this dimension would be correlated with changes in conflict of interest.

Perhaps several distinctions would be helpful in adding precision to the concept of conflictful behavior. One distinction is between acts that directly affect the substantive result of the interaction (such as a defection in the Prisoner's Dilemma) and acts that do not (such as verbal abuse in a bargaining situation). Another distinction that might be useful is between the amount of absolute as opposed to relative conflictful behavior of an act. For example, an act of verbal abuse can be thought of as representing some amount of absolute conflictful behavior in itself, but can also be regarded as representing an amount of relative conflictful behavior which depends upon the context of the interaction itself.

4. *Learn when the general hypothesis fails.* An understanding of the circumstances under which specific applications of the general hypothesis fail can be extremely valuable. Such failures can help refine the use of the concept of conflict of interest. For example, the examination of the coalitions in Italy that formed but were not minimal connected winning coalitions suggested several factors that could be included in a more comprehensive conflict of interest analysis of coalitions (8C). Such failures can also help identify what factors withstand analysis in terms of conflict of interest. For example, undirected hostility could not be explained in terms of conflict of interest because such behavior is independent of the particular strategic interaction.

5. *Integrate conflict of the interest with other theories.* This study has concentrated on the single concept of conflict of interest

not because of any hope that conflict of interest could explain every-thing, but rather because such a focus was helpful in developing the definition and applications for the concept.   In the long run the concept of conflict of interest can be most helpful when it is used in conjunction with other explanations of behavior.   Predictions based on several vari-ables are usually more accurate and realistic than those of any single-variable theory.   If several theories of behavior can be incorporated into a unified theory, the *ceteris paribus* assumption of each can be greatly relaxed and more complex situations can be analyzed.

F. Arenas of Application

Conflict of interest has been applied to four arenas of political activity in this study: bargaining in the Congressional conference com-mittee (5); the multilevel decisionmaking process in bureaucracies (6); consensus and cleavage in societies (7); and the coalition process in parliamentary democracies (8).   In each case the details of the institu-tional setting of the strategic interaction provided the structure needed for the construction of a model of the process.   In this sense the present study can be regarded as an example of "new institutionalism" as an approach to the study of politics.

An illustration of how conflict of interest can be used in the com-parative study of institutions is suggested by the basic theme that the more conflict of interest there is, the more likely is conflictful behavior. Suppose that in a given institution conflictful behavior is in fact propor-tional to conflict of interest.   Then the constant of proportionality represents the ability of that institution to manage conflict of interest. For example, if the ratio of conflictful behavior to conflict of interest is low in the Congressional conference committee then the conference committee is very successful at resolving conflict of interest because even a large amount of conflict of interest would not result in very much conflictful behavior.

Conflict of interest could also be applied to a number of topics in the study of international relations.   The example of bargaining over the terms of a treaty has already been mentioned (4A).   Some aspects of arms races and of military escalation could be analyzed in terms of the Prisoner's Dilemma played continuously over a period of time.   The amount of conflict of interest in such a Prisoner's Di-lemma might prove useful in the analysis of the direction and speed of these processes over time.

Conflict of interest analysis could be applied to other parts of the social sciences as well.   The present study has focused on political processes, but this does not reflect a limitation inherent in the concept of conflict of interest (1B).

Economics might be an especially fruitful field for the application of conflict of interest. For example, in industries dominated by a few firms, both collusion and price wars are possible. It is known that such oligopolistic interactions can be treated as n-person equivalents of the Prisoner's Dilemma. A detailed study of the size of the actual parameters in the game model could be used to yield estimates of the amount of conflict of interest in different industries at different times. Such estimates of conflict of interest could then in turn be used to predict (or explain) the relative amount of conflictful behavior between the firms. Another possible economic application is to the study of the bargaining process between labor and management. (A model quite similiar to the one used for bargaining between the House and Senate in the Congressional conference committee could be used (5).) Still another possible application of conflict of interest analysis is to the size of national tariffs, whether negotiated or arrived at by tacit interaction between nations.

Perhaps the most important application of conflict of interest in economics can be to the study of private and public goods. When two people have similar preferences for private goods (such as apples and oranges) there will be high conflict of interest. However when they have similar preferences for public goods (such as national defense and pollution control) there will be low conflict of interest. Conversely, dissimilar preferences for private goods yield low conflict of interest while dissimilar preferences for public goods yield high conflict of interest.

Other social science applications of conflict of interest might be made in the fields of psychology and sociology. For psychology, conflict of interest could be used as a control for environmental variables. It could also be used as a measuring rod for the propensity of an individual to exhibit characteristics such as "greed" and "trust," which can be defined in terms of specific behavior patterns in a game such as the Prisoner's Dilemma (see also 3B). For sociology, a conflict of interest analysis could be useful in the study of group behavior as exemplified by the processes of coalition formation and maintenance (see also 8A).

G. Policy Issues

Knowledge in the social sciences often has important implications for policy. Several of the considerations of conflict of interest that are relevant to policy issues can be briefly considered here. These considerations are meant to highlight a few important points, but they can hardly begin to suggest all the ways in which considerations of conflict of interest affect issues of policy.

1. *Conflict of interest is often low.*   Many, if not most, of the strategic interactions a person enters into have extremely low conflict of interest.   Quite frequently conflict of interest is so low that anything short of fully cooperative behavior would be absurd.   This point needs to be emphasized because attention is so often attracted by just those situations with an unusually large amount of conflict of interest.   The news media exemplify this tendency to focus upon the drama of high conflict of interest and conflictful behavior rather than the routine day-to-day interactions that are conducted smoothly.

Even when huge stakes are involved in a political arena, differences of view can sometimes be handled with a very high probability of success.   An example of this is the fact that the Senate and House conferees resolve their differences on 97% of the bills that come to the conference committee (5D).   The point that conflict of interest is often low or even negligible needs to be stressed just because it is often forgotten.

A related point is that even when conflict of interest is not low, it is rarely total.   Even wars are not zero-sum games, as shown by the fact that not everything that hurts one side helps the other.   One of the greatest contributions of game theory has been the appreciation that very few social interactions are zero-sum games.   Perhaps the specification of the dimension between partnership games and zero-sum games with the variable of conflict of interest will help bring this appreciation into sharper focus.

2. *Sometimes some conflict of interest is a good thing.*   Conflict of interest and the resulting conflictful behavior can be useful.   Both factors can help one of the parties to a dispute achieve and maintain group cohesion.   They can also help all the parties to a dispute recognize and begin to solve real problems they have, as Martin Luther King has pointed out (2E).   Conflict of interest can even help outsiders by encouraging competition among participants.   This last principle was institutionalized by the farmers of the American Constitution in their deliberate and successful efforts to promote conflict of interest between the President and Congress, and between the two chambers of Congress (2E).   A second example is the competition between political parties which can help the voter (8).   Still another example is provided by the capitalist system which, in the ideal case, has so

much conflict of interest between numerous firms in each industry that collusion is impossible, much to the benefit of the consumer.

3. *Conflict of interest can be altered.*   The geometric and parametric analyses used throughout this study suggest a great many ways in which conflict of interest in a given situation can be increased or decreased.

Technology, in its broadest sense, can change the amount of conflict of interest by providing new strategy choices for the participants. Thus, for example, if people caught in a Prisoner's Dilemma are given the additional strategy choices associated with making their choices of cooperation or defection conditional upon the other's choice, the conflict of interest disappears.   (The idea is due to Nigel Howard.   See Rapoport, 1967b for details.)   Of course, the invention or discovery of new feasible agreements in a bargaining game is another example of how the amount of conflict of interest can change (2E).

In some cases the opportunity for choice is quite clear.   For example, the drawing of boundaries for legislative districts affects the conflict of interest in both legislative elections and the legislature itself (7C).   How these boundaries will be drawn is a matter of choice; it is a type of "political engineering."

Since conflict of interest is not immutable, and since the amount of conflict of interest can have important consequences, wisdom in its manipulation is needed.

Bibliography

Ackoff, Russell L. *Model Study of Escalation, Project Philosophy and Program.* Preliminary Report, Arms Control and Disarmament Agency ST-64, Technical Paper #041265 (mimeo), 1965.

Adams, John Clarke, and Barile, Paolo. *The Government of Republican Italy.* Boston: Houghton Mifflin, 1961.

Argyris, Chris. *Understanding Organizational Behavior.* Homewood, Ill.: Dorsey Press, 1960.

——————. *Interpersonal Competence and Organizational Effectiveness.* Homewood, Ill.: Dorsey Press, 1962.

Aristotle. *The Athenian Constitution, The Eudemian Ethics, On Vices and Virtues.* Translated by H. Rackam. Cambridge, Mass.: Harvard Univ. Press, 1938.

——————. *The Politics of Aristotle.* Translated by Ernest Barker. New York: Oxford Univ. Press, 1962.

Aubert, Vilhelm. "Competition and Dissensus: Two Types of Conflict and of Conflict Resolution." *Journal of Conflict Resolution,* 7 (1963), 26–42.

Axelrod, Robert. "Conflict of Interest: An Axiomatic Approach." *Journal of Conflict Resolution,* 11 (1967a), 87–99.

——————. "The Structure of Public Opinion on Policy Issues." *Public Opinion Quarterly,* 31 (1967b), 51–60.

Bachrach, Peter, and Baratz, Morton S. "Decisions and Non-decisions: An Analytic Framework." *American Political Science Review,* 57 (1963), 632–642.

Barnes, Samuel H. "Italy: Oppositions on Left, Right and Center," in Robert Dahl, ed., *Political Oppositions in Western Democracies.* New Haven, Conn.: Yale Univ. Press, 1966, pp. 303–331 and 435.

Berelson, Bernard, and Steiner, Gary A. *Human Behavior.* New York: Harcourt, Brace & World, 1964.

——————; Lazarsfeld, Paul F.; and McPhee, William N. *Voting*. Chicago: Univ. of Chicago Press, 1954.

Bernard, Jessie. "The Sociological Study of Conflict," in International Sociological Association, *The Nature of Conflict*. Paris, 1957, pp. 33–117.

Black, Duncan. *The Theory of Committees and Elections*. Cambridge, England: Cambridge Univ. Press, 1958.

Boulding, Kenneth E. "The Economics of Human Conflict," in Elton B. McNeil, ed., *The Nature of Human Conflict*. Englewood Cliffs, N.J.: Prentice-Hall, 1965, pp. 172–191.

Bury, J. B. *A History of Greece to the Death of Alexander the Great*. 2nd ed. London: Macmillan, 1913.

Campbell, Angus; Converse, Phillip E.; Miller, Warren E.; and Stokes, Donald E. *The American Voter*. New York: Wiley, 1960.

Chamberlain, Joseph P. *Legislative Processes, National and State*. New York: Appleton-Century, 1936.

Churchman, C. West. *Prediction and Optimal Decision*. Englewood Cliffs, N.J.: Prentice-Hall, 1961.

Coser, Lewis. *The Functions of Social Conflict*. New York: Free Press of Glencoe, 1956.

Cyert, Richard M., and March, James G. *A Behavioral Theory of the Firm*. Englewood Cliffs, N.J.: Prentice-Hall, 1963.

Dahl, Robert A. *A Preface to Democratic Theory*. Chicago: Univ. of Chicago Press, 1956.

——————. *Modern Political Analysis*. Englewood Cliffs, N.J.: Prentice-Hall, 1963.

——————. *Pluralist Democracy in the United States: Conflict and Consent*. Chicago: Rand McNally, 1967.

Dahrendorf, Ralf. *Class and Class Conflict in Industrial Society*. Stanford, Calif.: Stanford Univ. Press, 1959.

Davis, Otto A., and Hinich, Melvin J. "A Mathematical Model of Policy Formation in a Democratic Society," in Joseph L. Bernd, ed., *Mathematical Applications in Political Science, II*. Dallas: Arnold Foundation, 1966, pp. 175–208.

DeSwaan, Abraham. "An Empirical Model of Cabinet Formation as an *n*-Person Game of Policy Distance Minimization," in Sven Groennings, E. W. Kelly, and Michael A. Leiserson, eds., *The Study of Coalition Behavior*. New York: Holt, Rinehart and Winston, forthcoming.

Deutsch, Karl W. "The Limits of Common Sense," *Psychiatry*, 22 (1959), 105–112. Reprinted in Nelson W. Polsby, Robert A. Dentler, and Paul A. Smith, eds., *Politics and Social Life*. Boston: Houghton Mifflin, 1963, pp. 51–58.

——————. *The Nerves of Government.* New York: Free Press of Glencoe, 1963.

——————. "Power and Communication in International Society," in Anthony de Reuck and Julie Knight, eds., *Conflict in Society.* Boston: Little, Brown, 1966, pp. 300–316.

Deutsch, Morton. "A Theory of Co-operation and Competition." *Human Relations,* 2 (1949), 129–152.

Downs, Anthony. *An Economic Theory of Democracy.* New York: Harper & Row, 1957.

——————. *Inside Bureaucracy.* Boston: Little, Brown, 1967.

Easton, David. *A Systems Analysis of Political Life.* New York: Wiley, 1965.

Fenno, Richard F., Jr. "The Appropriations Committee as a Political System," in Robert L. Peabody and Nelson W. Polsby, eds., *New Perspectives on the House of Representatives.* Chicago: Rand McNally, 1963, pp. 79–108. Reprinted from "The House Appropriations Committee as a Political System: The Problem of Integration." *American Political Science Review,* 56 (1962), 310–324.

——————. *The Power of the Purse.* Boston: Little, Brown, 1966.

Galloway, George B. *Congress at the Crossroads.* New York: Crowell, 1946.

Gross, Bertram. *The Legislative Struggle.* New York: McGraw-Hill, 1953.

Harris, Richard J. "A Geometric Classification System for 2×2 Interval-Symmetric Games." *Behavioral Science,* 14 (1969), 138–146.

Harsanyi, John C. "Some Social Science Implications of a New Approach to Game Theory," in Kathleen Archibald, ed., *Strategic Interaction and Conflict.* Berkeley: Univ. of California, 1966, pp. 1–18.

Hitch, Charles J., and McKean, Roland N. *The Economics of Defense in the Nuclear Age.* Cambridge, Mass.: Harvard Univ. Press, 1960.

Hotelling, Harold. "Stability in Competition." *The Economic Journal,* 39 (1929), 41–57.

Huntington, Samuel P. *The Common Defense.* New York: Columbia Univ. Press, 1961.

"An Individual Who Happens to Be a Negro." *Time,* 89 (1967), 20–23.

Kaplan, Abraham. *The Conduct of Inquiry.* San Francisco: Chandler, 1964.

Keesing's Contemporary Archives. London: Keesing's Ltd., Vol. 6–16 (1946–1968).

Key, V. O., Jr. *Politics, Parties, and Pressure Groups.* 5th ed. New York: Crowell, 1964.

King, Martin Luther, Jr. "A Letter From Birmingham Jail." *Ebony,* 18 (August, 1963), 22–33.

Kogan, Norman. *The Government of Italy.* New York: Crowell, 1962.

Lasswell, Harold D. *Psychopathology and Politics.* Chicago: Univ. of Chicago Press, 1930.

——————. "Conflict, Social." *Encyclopaedia of the Social Sciences,* 4 (1931), 194–196.

Lave, Lester B. "Factors Affecting Co-operation in the Prisoner's Dilemma." *Behavioral Science,* 10 (1965), 26–38.

Leiserson, Michael A. *Coalitions in Politics.* Ph.D. Dissertation, New Haven, Conn.: Yale Univ. (mimeo), 1966.

——————. "Factions and Coalitions in One-Party Japan: An Interpretation Based on the Theory of Games." *American Political Science Review,* 62 (1968), 770–787.

Lijphart, Arend. *The Politics of Accommodation.* Berkeley: Univ. of California Press, 1968.

Lindblom, Charles E. *The Intelligence of Democracy.* New York: Free Press of Glencoe, 1965.

Luce, R. Duncan, and Raiffa, Howard. *Games and Decisions.* New York: Wiley, 1957.

Lutzker, Daniel R. "Internationalism as a Predictor of Cooperative Behavior." *Journal of Conflict Resolution,* 4 (1960), 426–430.

Madison, James. "The Federalist No. 10." 1787.

March, James G., and Simon, Herbert A. *Organizations.* New York: Wiley, 1958.

May, Mark A., and Doob, Leonard W. *Competition and Cooperation.* New York: Social Science Research Council, Bulletin Number 25, 1937.

Mayo, H. B. *An Introduction to Democratic Theory.* New York: Oxford Univ. Press, 1960.

McCown, Ada C. *The Congressional Conference Committee,* New York: Columbia Univ. Press, 1927.

Nash, John F., Jr. "The Bargaining Problem." *Econometrica,* 18 (1950), 155–162.

Neustadt, Richard E. *Presidential Power.* New York: Wiley, 1960.

Olson, Mancur, Jr. *The Logic of Collective Action.* Cambridge Mass.: Harvard Univ. Press, 1965.

Oskamp, Stuart, and Perlman, Daniel. "Factors Affecting Cooperation in a Prisoner's Dilemma Game." *Journal of Conflict Resolution,* 9 (1965), 359–374.

Porsholt, Lars. "On Methods of Conflict Prevention." *Journal of Peace Research,* 1966, 179–193.

Pressman, Jeffrey L. *House vs. Senate.* New Haven, Conn.: Yale Univ. Press, 1966.

Pruit, Dean G. "Reward Structure and Its Effect on Cooperation." Newark, Del.: Center for Research on Social Behavior, Univ. of Delaware (mimeo), 1965.

Pye, Lucian W. *Politics, Personality, and Nation Building.* New Haven, Conn.: Yale Univ. Press, 1962.

Rapoport, Anatol. "Some Self-Organizing Parameters in Three-Person Groups." *General Systems,* 5 (1960), 129–143.

——————. *Strategy and Conscience.* New York: Harper & Row, 1964.

——————. "A Note on the 'Index of Cooperation' for Prisoner's Dilemma." *Journal of Conflict Resolution,* 11 (1967a), 100–103.

——————. "Escape from Paradox." *Scientific American,* 217 (July, 1967b), 50–56.

——————, and Chammah, Albert M. *Prisoner's Dilemma.* Ann Arbor: Univ. of Michigan Press, 1965.

——————; ——————; Dwyer, John; and Gyr, John. "Three-Person Non-Zero-Sum Nonnegotiable Games." *Behavioral Science,* 7 (1962), 38–58.

——————, and Orwant, Carol. "Experimental Games: A Review." *Behavioral Science,* 7 (1962), 1–37.

Rappoport, Leon H. "Interpersonal Conflict in Cooperative and Uncertain Situations." *Journal of Experimental Social Psychology,* 1 (1965), 323–333.

Reich, Utz-Peter. "Conflict of Interest: A Pragmatic Approach." *Journal of Peace Research,* (1968, no. 2), 211–215.

Riker, William H. *The Theory of Political Coalitions.* New Haven, Conn.: Yale Univ. Press, 1962.

Rosenthal, Howard. "Simulating Elections in Western Democracies." Pittsburgh, Penna.: Carnegie Institute of Technology (mimeo), 1967.

Ross, Edward Alsworth. *The Principles of Sociology.* New York: Century, 1920.

Rousseau, Jean Jacques. *The Social Contract and Discourses.* Translated by G. D. H. Cole. New York: Dutton, 1950.

Sampson, Anthony. *Anatomy of Britain Today.* New York: Harper & Row, 1965.

Sampson, Edward E., and Kardush, Marcelle. "Age, Sex, Class and Race Differences in Response to a Two-Person, Non-Zero-Sum Game." *Journal of Conflict Resolution*, 9 (1965), 212–220.

Sartori, Giovanni. "European Political Parties: The Case of Polarized Pluralism," in Joseph LaPalombara and Myron Weiner, eds., *Political Parties and Political Development*. Princeton, N.J.: Princeton Univ. Press, 1966, pp. 137–176.

Sawyer, Jack, and Guetzkow, Harold. "Bargaining and Negotiations in International Relations," in Herbert C. Kelman, ed., *International Behavior: A Social-Psychological Analysis*. New York: Holt, Rinehart and Winston, 1965, pp. 466–520.

Schelling, Thomas C. *The Strategy of Conflict*. Cambridge, Mass.: Harvard Univ. Press, 1960.

Shannon, Claude, and Weaver, Warren. *The Mathematical Theory of Communication*. Urbana: Univ. of Illinois Press, 1949.

Simmel, Georg. *Conflict*. Translated by Kurt H. Wolff. Glencoe, Ill.: Free Press, 1955.

Snyder, Richard C.; Bruck, H. W.; and Sapin, Burton. *Foreign Policy Decision-Making*. New York: Free Press of Glencoe, 1962.

Starbuck, William. "Mathematics and Organization Theory," in James G. March, ed., *Handbook of Organizations*. Chicago: Rand McNally, 1965.

Steiner, Gilbert Y. *The Congressional Conference Committee*. Urbana: Univ. of Illinois Press, Illinois Studies in the Social Sciences, 32 (1951).

Stokes, Donald E. "Spatial Models of Party Competition." *American Political Science Review*, 57 (1963), 368–377.

Temperley, Harold W. V. *Senates and Upper Chambers*. London: Chapman and Hall, 1910.

Tullock, Gordon. *The Politics of Bureaucracy*. Washington, D.C.: Public Affairs Press, 1965.

—————. *Toward a Mathematics of Politics*. Ann Arbor: Univ. of Michigan Press, 1967.

Twain, Mark. *The Adventures of Tom Sawyer*. New York: New American Library, 1959 (originally published in 1876).

Valavanis, Stefan. "The Resolution of Conflict When Utilities Interact." *Journal of Conflict Resolution*, 2 (1958), 156–169.

Von Neumann, John, and Morgenstern, Oskar. *Theory of Games and Economic Behavior*. 2nd ed. Princeton, N.J.: Princeton Univ. Press, 1947.

Wildavsky, Aaron. *The Politics of the Budgetary Process*. Boston: Little, Brown, 1964.

Index